EASY GUITAR
WITH NOTES & TAB

JAZZ CLASSICS
FOR EASY GUITAR

ISBN 978-1-4950-7188-1

7777 W. BLUEMOUND RD. P.O. BOX 13819 MILWAUKEE, WI 53213

Visit Hal Leonard Online at
www.halleonard.com

As Time Goes By

from CASABLANCA

Words and Music by Herman Hupfeld

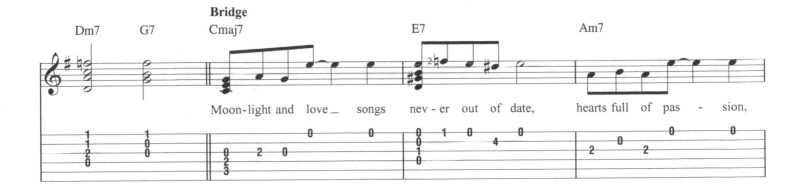

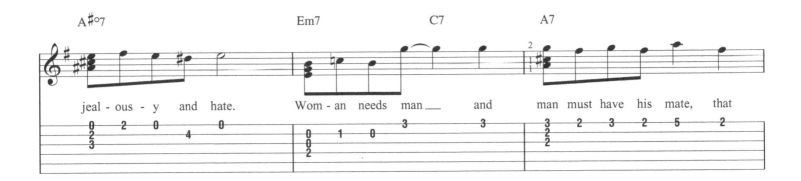

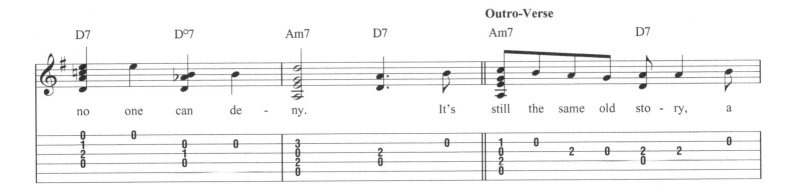

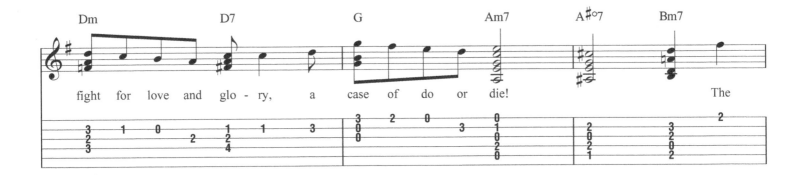

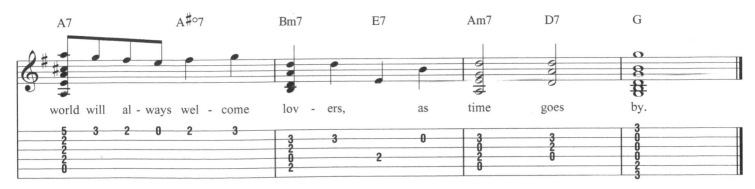

At Last

from ORCHESTRA WIVES

Lyric by Mack Gordon
Music by Harry Warren

Strum Pattern: 3
Pick Pattern: 3

Verse
Moderately slow

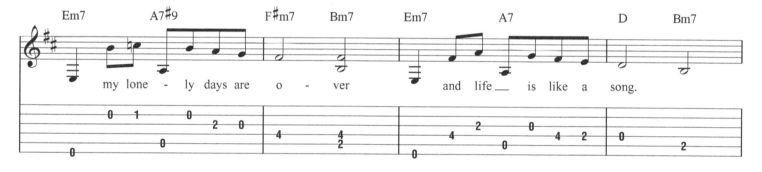

At last my love___ has come a - long,
my lone - ly days are o - ver and life___ is like a song.

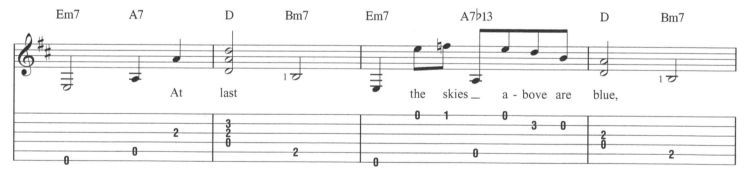

At last the skies___ a - bove are blue,
my heart___ was wrapped in clo - ver the night___ I looked at you.

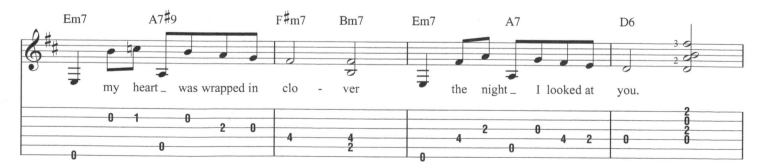

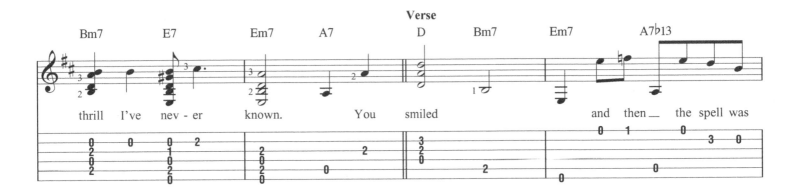

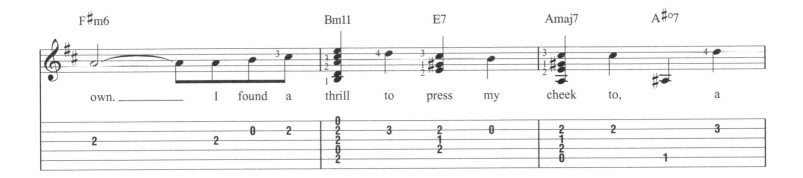

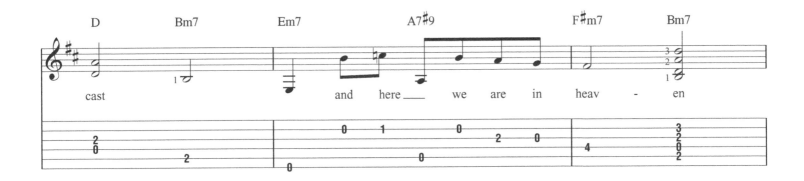

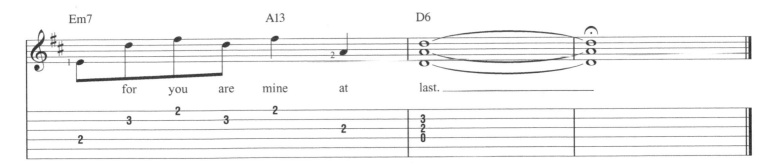

The Best Is Yet to Come

Music by Cy Coleman
Lyrics by Carolyn Leigh

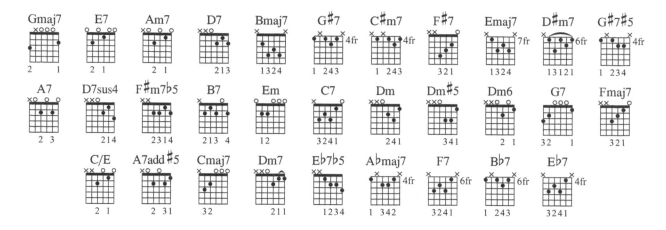

*Capo I

Strum Pattern: 4
Pick Pattern: 3

*Optional: To match recording, place capo at 1st fret.

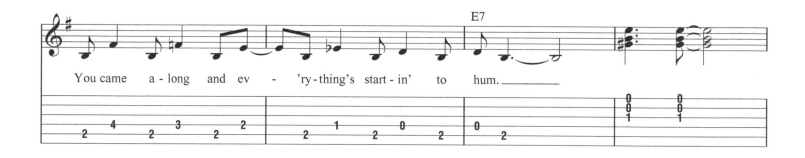

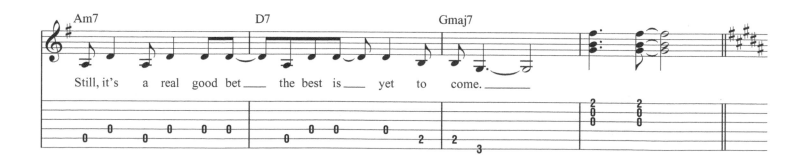

Verse

2. The best is yet to come, _ and babe, won't it be fine? _____

You think you've seen the sun, _ but you ain't seen it shine. _____ Wait 'til the warm-up's

un-der-way, _ wait till our lips have met. _ Wait 'til you see that sun-shine day, _

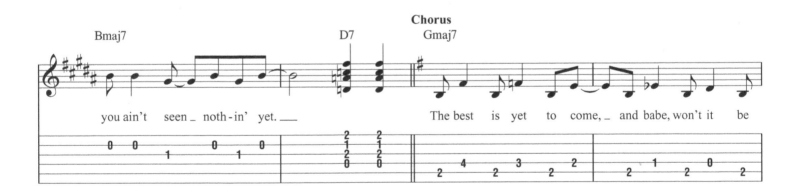

Chorus

you ain't seen _ noth-in' yet. _ The best is yet to come, _ and babe, won't it be

fine? _____ The best is yet to come, _ come the day _ you're mine, _____

come the day you're mine, _____ I'm gon - na teach you to fly. _____

We've on - ly tast - ed the wine. _____ We're gon - na drain the cup dry. _____

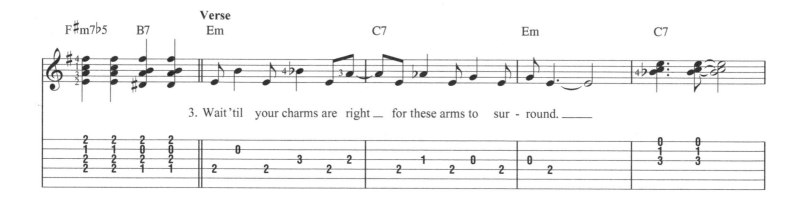

Verse

3. Wait 'til your charms are right _ for these arms to sur - round. _____

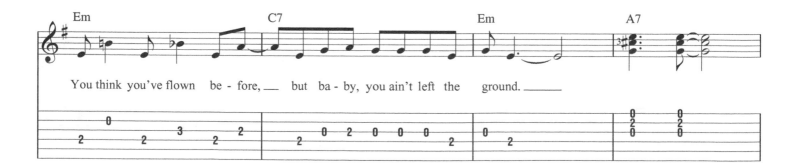

You think you've flown be - fore, _ but ba - by, you ain't left the ground. _____

But Not for Me

from GIRL CRAZY

Music and Lyrics by George Gershwin and Ira Gershwin

Strum Pattern: 5
Pick Pattern: 1

Verse

Moderately fast

1. They're writ-ing songs of love ___ but not for me.
3. *See additional lyrics*

A luck-y star's a-bove ___ but not for me. With love to

lead the way ___ I've found more clouds of gray ___ than an-y

Rus-sian play ___ could guar-an-tee.

2. I was a
4. *See additional lyrics*

Additional Lyrics

3. He's knocking on a door, but not for me.
   He'll plan a two by four, but not for me.
   I know that love's a game; I'm puzzled, just the same.
   Was I the moth or flame? I'm all at sea.

4. It all began so well, but what an end!
   This is the time a feller needs a friend,
   When ev'ry happy plot ends with the marriage knot,
   And there's no knot for me.

Bye Bye Blackbird

from PETE KELLY'S BLUES

Words by Mort Dixon
Music by Ray Henderson

Chorus

No one here can love and un-der-stand me.

Oh, what hard luck sto-ries they all hand me.

Verse

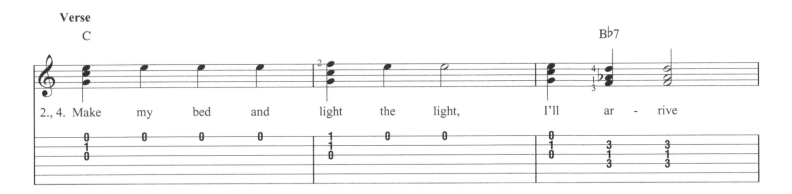

2., 4. Make my bed and light the light, I'll ar-rive

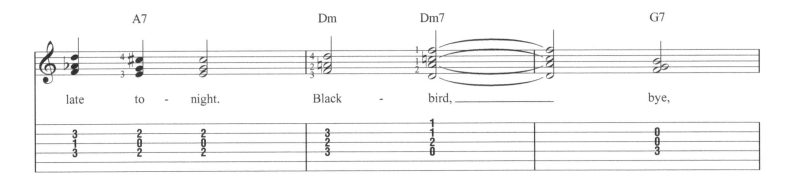

late to-night. Black-bird, _____ bye,

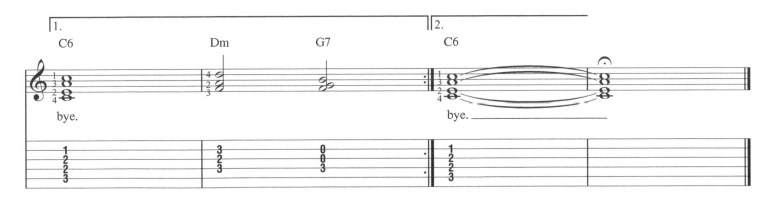

1. bye.   2. bye. _____

Caravan

Words and Music by Duke Ellington, Irving Mills and Juan Tizol

Strum Pattern: 3
Pick Pattern: 3

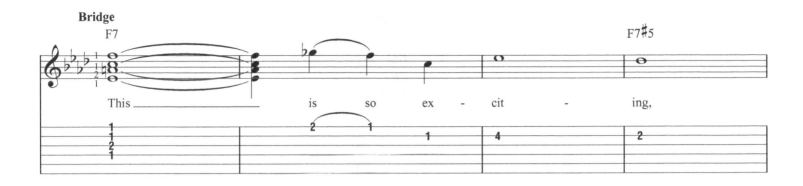

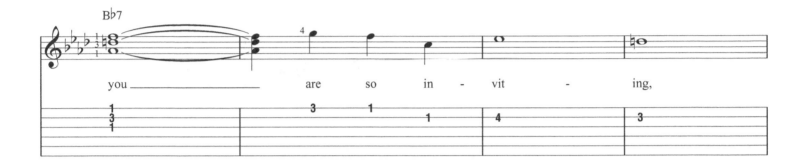

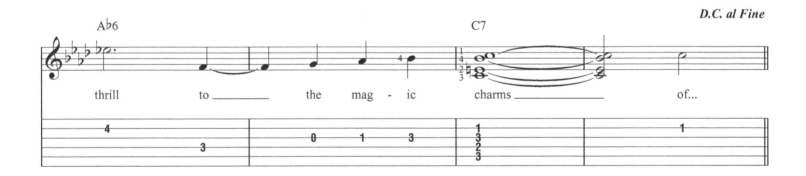

Additional Lyrics

2. Sleep upon my shoulder as we creep
   Across the sands so I may keep
   This memory of our caravan.

3. ...You, beside me here beneath the blue,
   My dream of love is coming true
   Within our desert caravan.

Charade

from CHARADE

Music by Henry Mancini
Words by Johnny Mercer

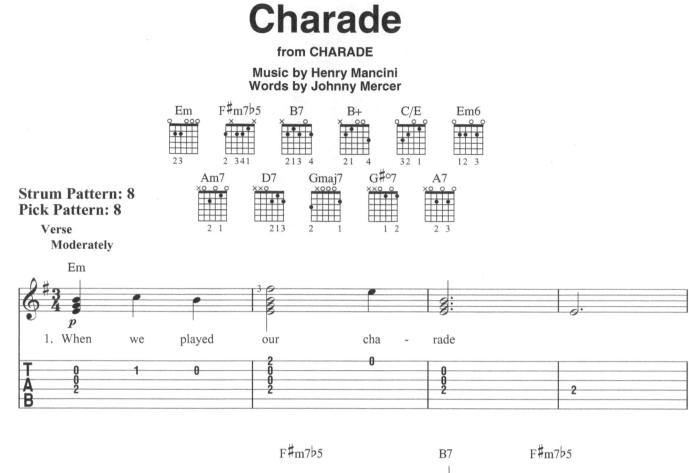

Strum Pattern: 8
Pick Pattern: 8

Verse
Moderately

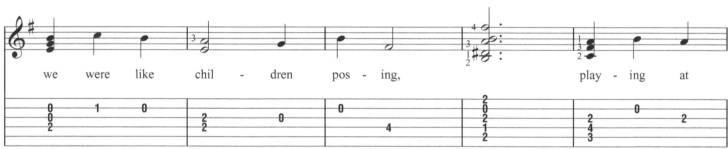

When we played our cha - rade

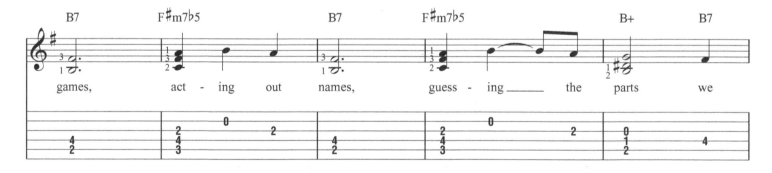

we were like chil - dren pos - ing, play - ing at

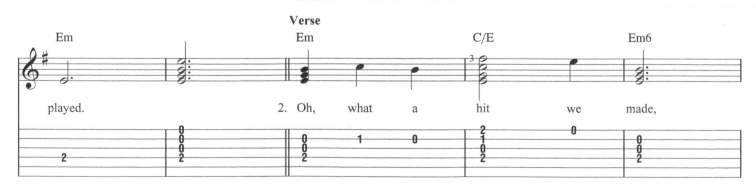

games, act - ing out names, guess - ing _____ the parts we

played. 2. Oh, what a hit we made,

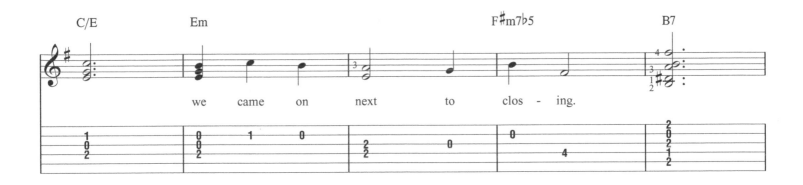

we came on next to clos - ing.

Best on the bill, lov - ers un - til love left _____ the

Bridge

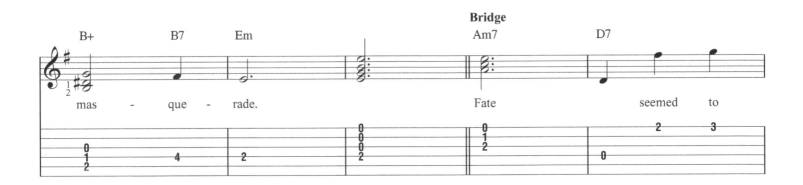

mas - que - rade. Fate seemed to

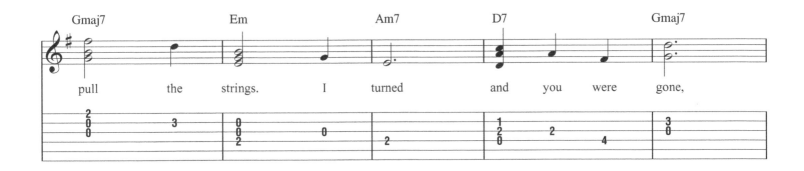

pull the strings. I turned and you were gone,

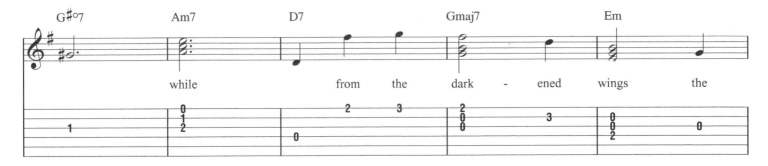

while from the dark - ened wings the

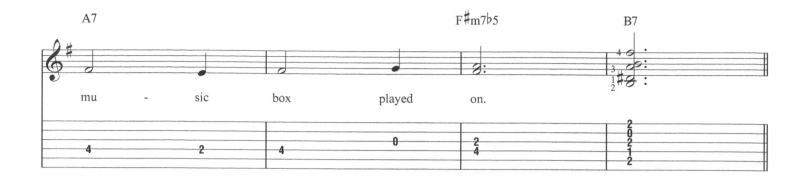

mu - sic box played on.

Verse

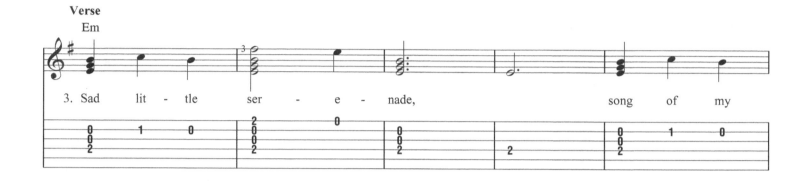

3. Sad lit - tle ser - e - nade, song of my

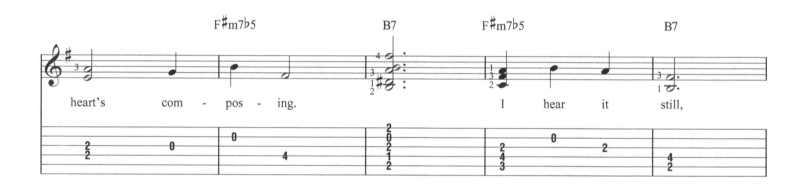

heart's com - pos - ing. I hear it still,

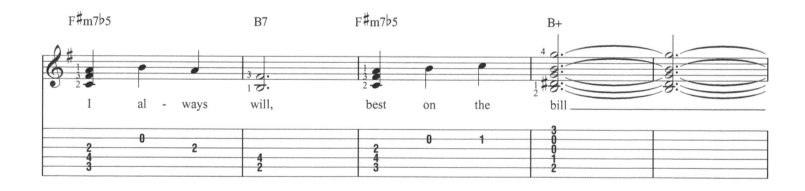

I al - ways will, best on the bill _____

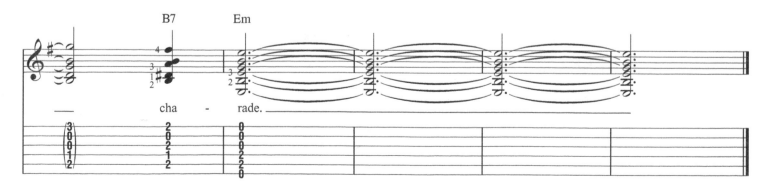

_____ cha - rade. _____

Estate

Music by Bruno Martino
Lyrics by Bruno Brighetti

Am7 Dm7 E7 G13 Cmaj7 Fmaj7

Bm11 Bb7 E7#5 Amaj7 Bm7 E7#9

Strum Pattern: 5
Pick Pattern: 5

Verse
Moderately slow

1. E - (3.)sta - te _____ sei cal - da co - me i ba - ci che ho per - du - to _____ sei

pie - na di un a - mo - re che è pas - sa - to _____ che il cuo - re mio vor - reb - be can - cel -

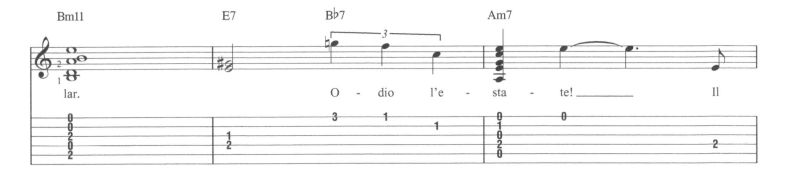

lar. O - dio l'e - sta - te! _____ Il

so - le che o - gni gior - no ci scal - da - va, _____ che splen - di - di tra - mon - ti di - pin -

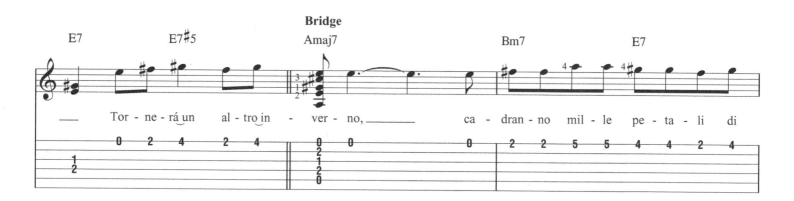

ge - va _____ a - des - so bru - cia so - lo con fu - ror. _____

Bridge

__ Tor - ne - rá un al - tro in - ver - no, _____ ca - dran - no mil - le pe - ta - li di

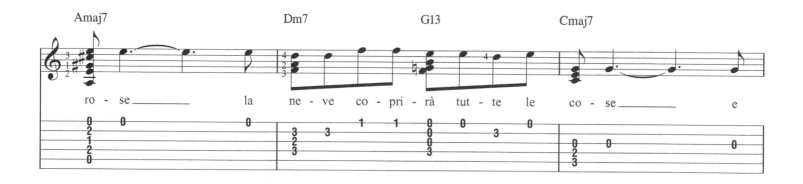

ro - se _____ la ne - ve co - pri - rà tut - te le co - se _____ e

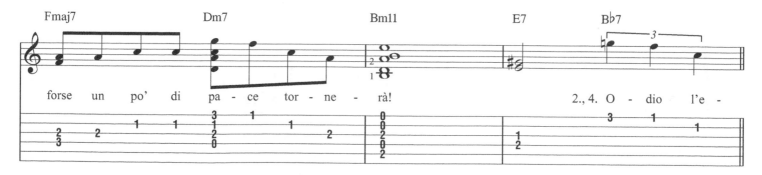

for - se un po' di pa - ce tor - ne - rà! 2., 4. O - dio l'e -

Verse

sta - te _____ che ha da - to il suo pro - fu - mo ad o - gni fio - re, _____ l'e -

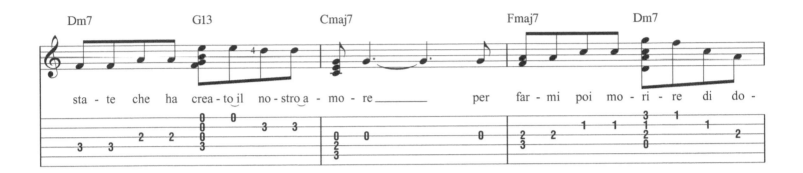

sta - te che ha crea - to il no - stro a - mo - re _____ per far - mi poi mo - ri - re di do -

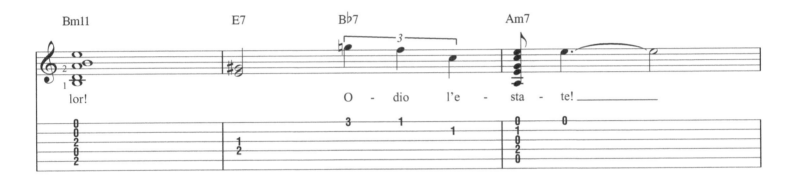

lor! O - dio l'e - sta - te! _____

1.

O - dio l'e - sta - te! _____ 3. E -

2.

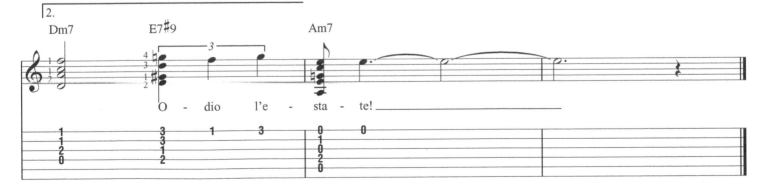

O - dio l'e - sta - te! _____

21

A Child Is Born

Music by Thad Jones
Lyrics by Alec Wilder

Strum Pattern: 7
Pick Pattern: 7

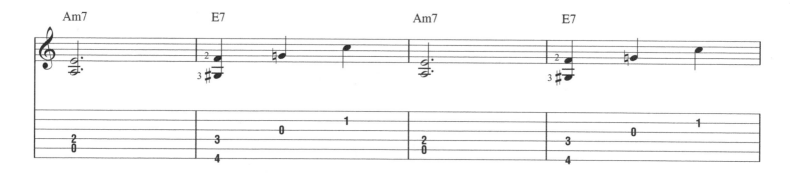

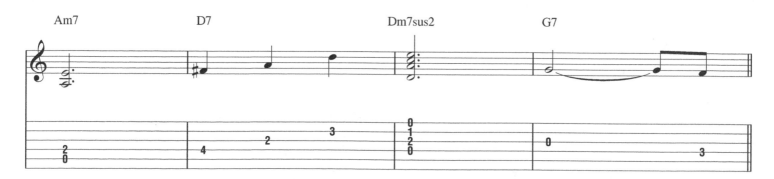

B

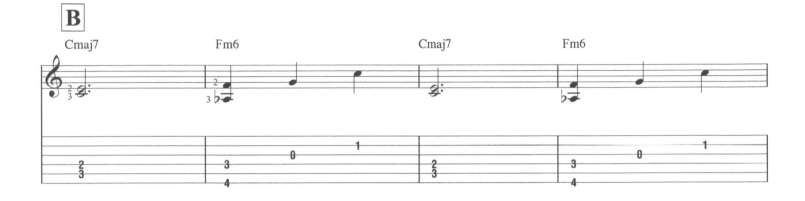

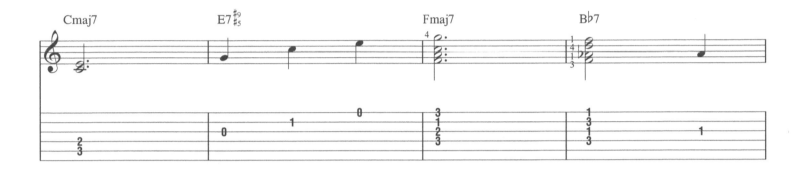

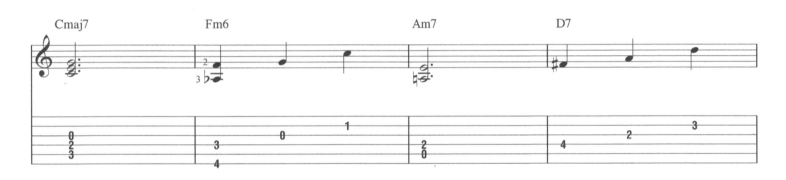

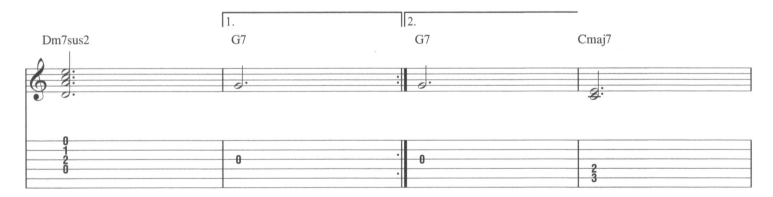

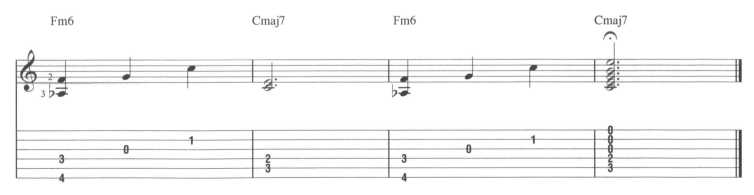

Cute

Music by Neal Hefti
Words by Stanley Styne

Strum Pattern: 3
Pick Pattern: 3

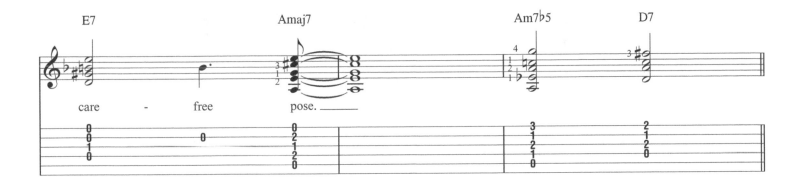

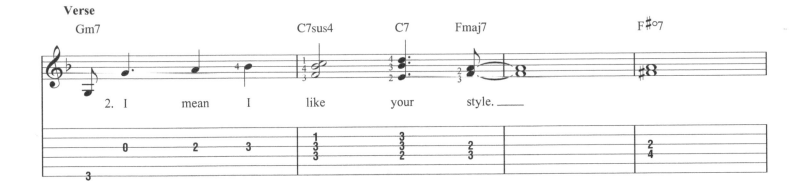

Verse

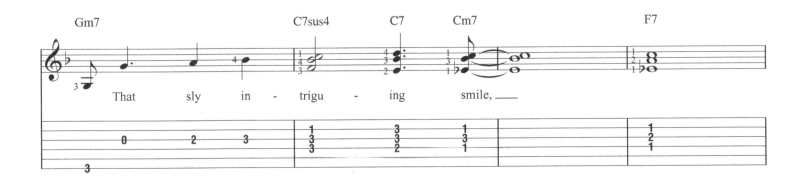

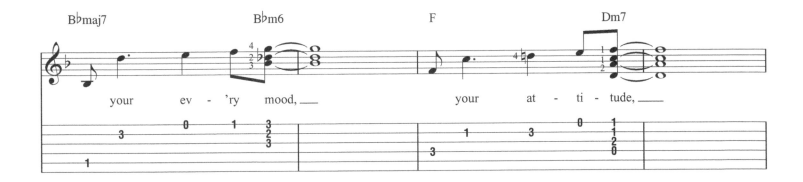

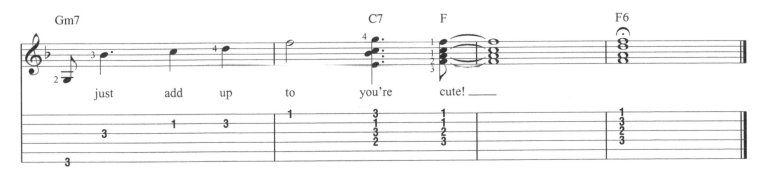

Days of Wine and Roses

from DAYS OF WINE AND ROSES

Lyrics by Johnny Mercer
Music by Henry Mancini

Strum Pattern: 3
Pick Pattern: 3

lone - ly night dis - clos - es just a

pass - ing breeze filled with mem - o - ries

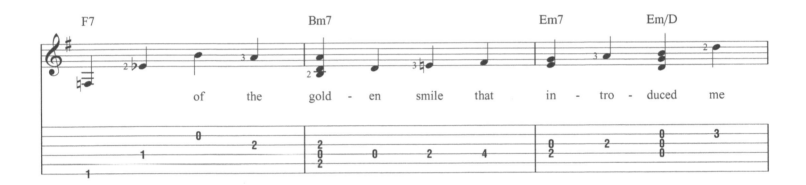

of the gold - en smile that in - tro - duced me

to the days of wine and

ros - es and you. 2. The

Do Nothin' Till You Hear from Me

Words and Music by Duke Ellington and Bob Russell

Strum Pattern: 5
Pick Pattern: 1

Verse

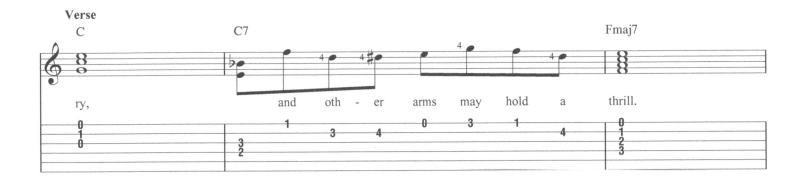

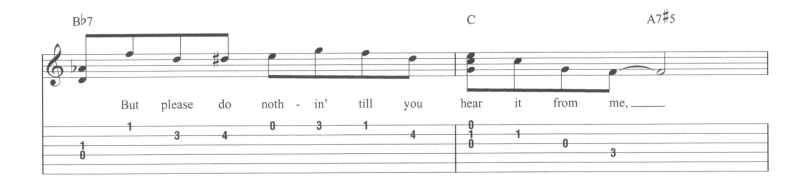

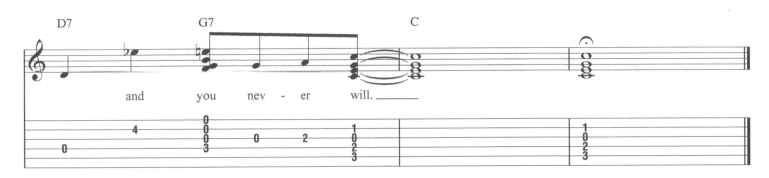

Easy to Love
(You'd Be So Easy to Love)

from BORN TO DANCE
Words and Music by Cole Porter

Strum Pattern: 3
Pick Pattern: 3

Verse

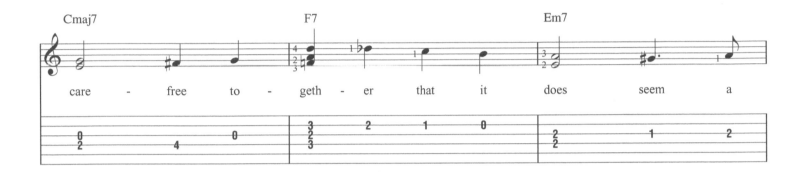

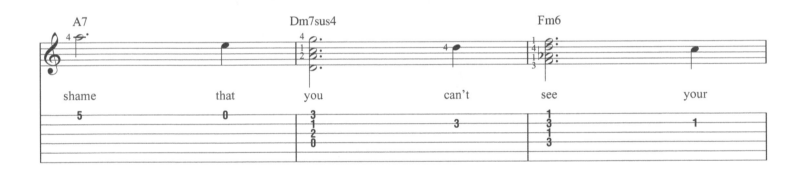

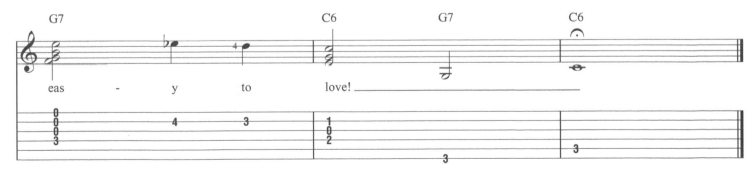

Embraceable You

from CRAZY FOR YOU

Music and Lyrics by George Gershwin and Ira Gershwin

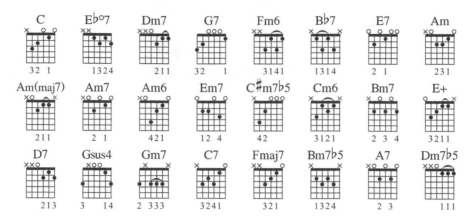

Strum Pattern: 3
Pick Pattern: 1

Verse
Moderately fast

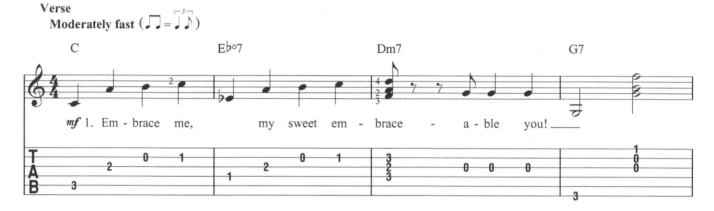

1. Em - brace me, my sweet em - brace - a - ble you! _____

Em - brace me, you ir - re - place - a - ble you! _____

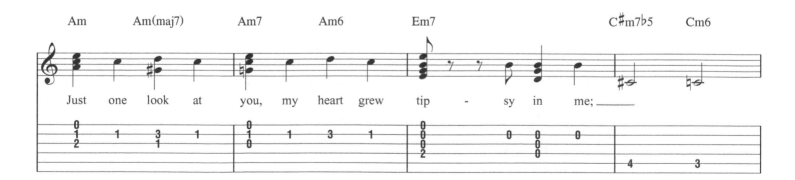

Just one look at you, my heart grew tip - sy in me; _____

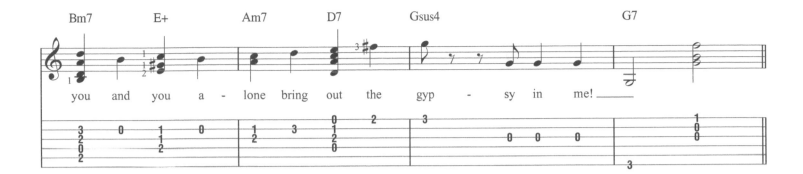

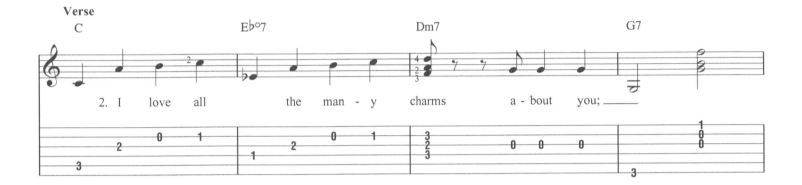

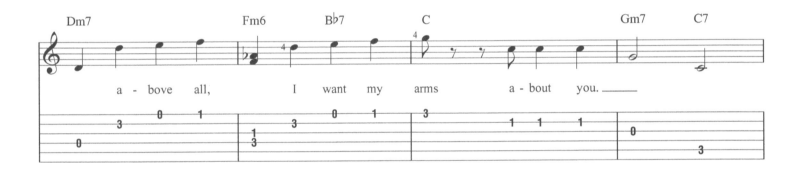

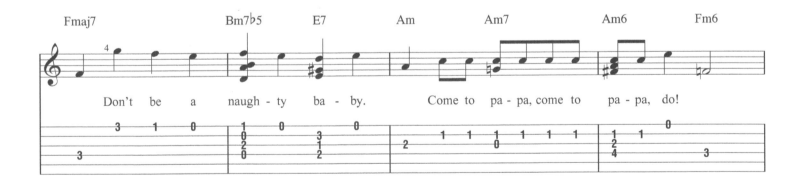

Emily

from the MGM Motion Picture THE AMERICANIZATION OF EMILY

Music by Johnny Mandel
Words by Johnny Mercer

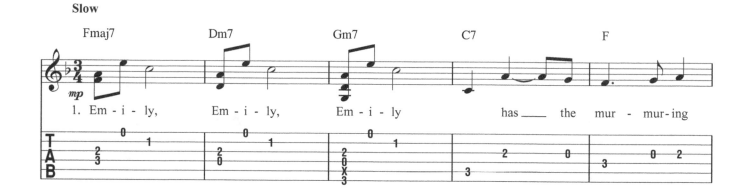

Strum Pattern: 7
Pick Pattern: 7

Verse
Slow

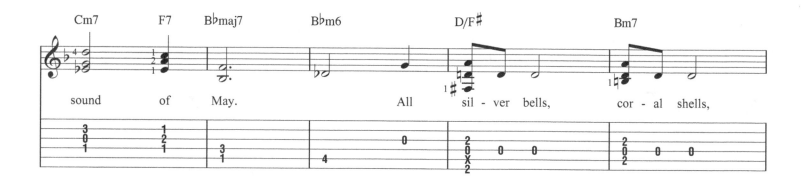

1. Em - i - ly, Em - i - ly, Em - i - ly has ___ the mur - mur - ing

sound of May. All sil - ver bells, cor - al shells,

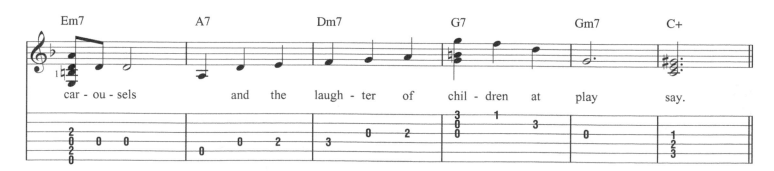

car - ou - sels and the laugh - ter of chil - dren at play say.

Verse

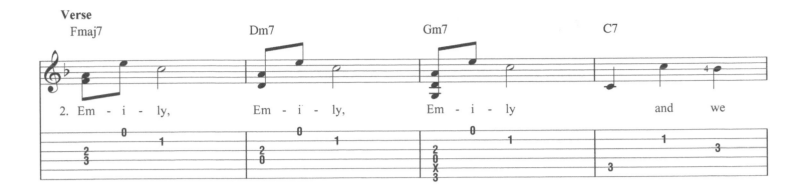

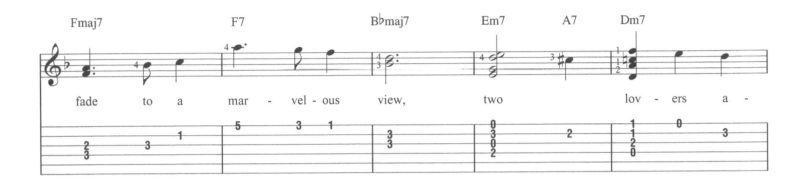

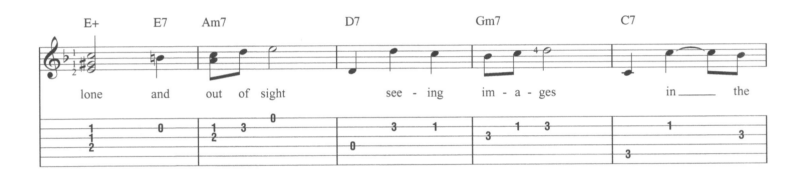

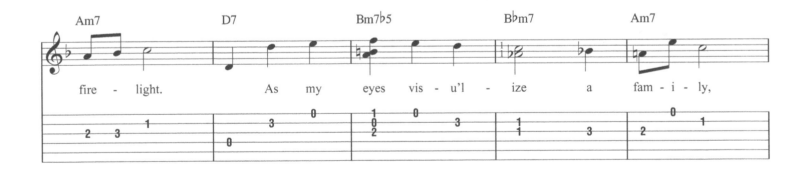

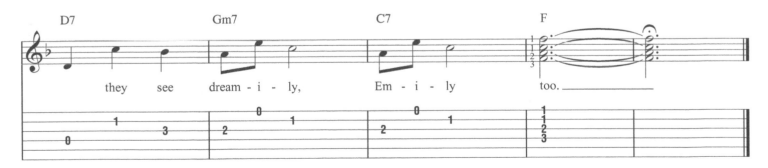

Fascinating Rhythm

from RHAPSODY IN BLUE

Music and Lyrics by George Gershwin and Ira Gershwin

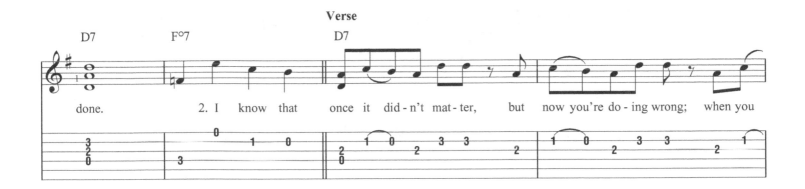

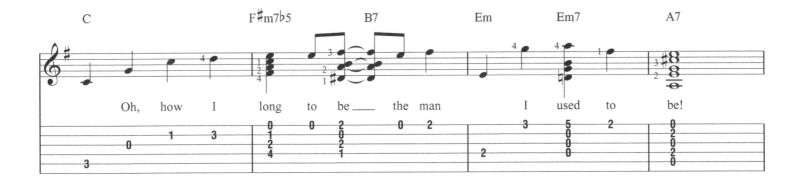

A Foggy Day (In London Town)

from A DAMSEL IN DISTRESS
Music and Lyrics by George Gershwin and Ira Gershwin

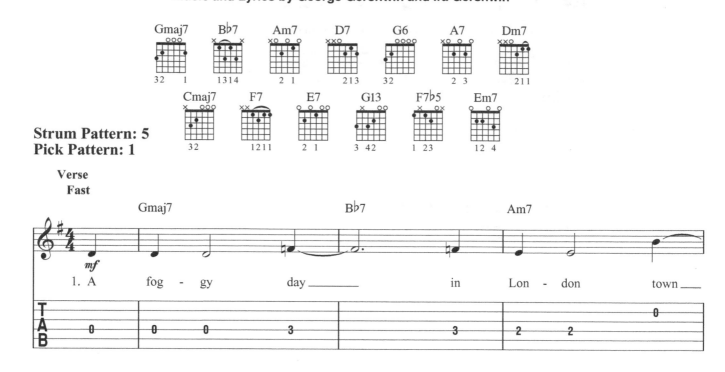

Strum Pattern: 5
Pick Pattern: 1

Verse
Fast

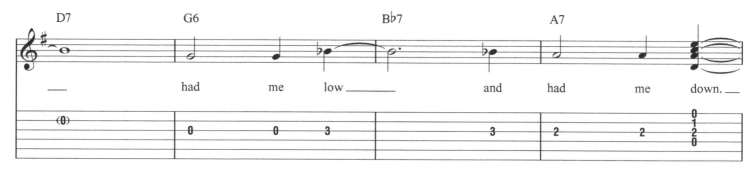

1. A fog-gy day _____ in Lon-don town _____

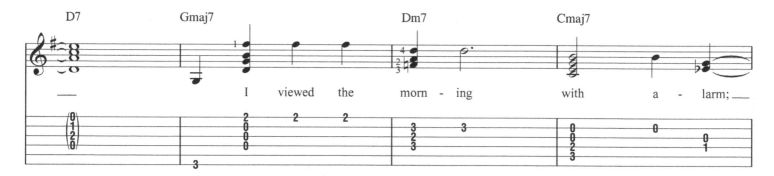

_____ had me low _____ and had me down. _____

I viewed the morn-ing with a-larm; _____

_____ the Brit-ish Mu-se-um had lost its charm. _____

Verse

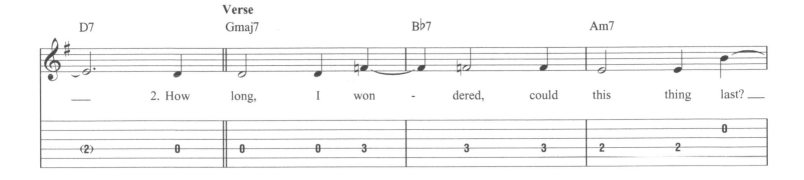

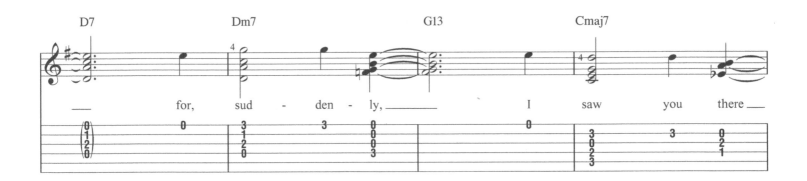

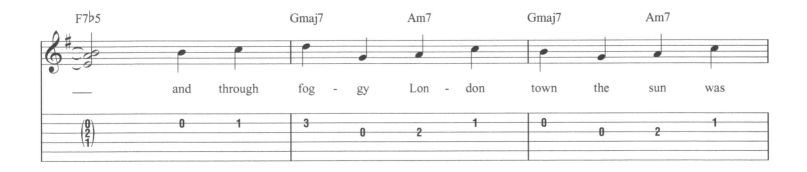

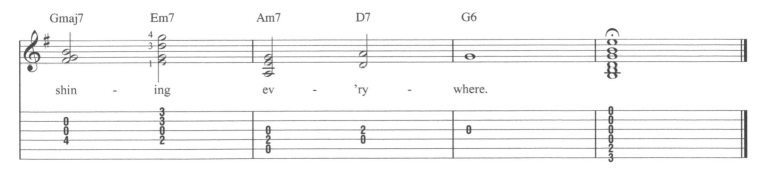

Gentle Rain

from the Motion Picture THE GENTLE RAIN

Music by Luiz Bonfa
Words by Matt Dubey

Strum Pattern: 5
Pick Pattern: 5

Verse
Moderately

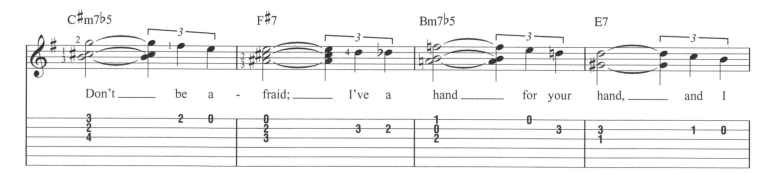

1. We ___ both are lost ___ and a - lone ___ in the world; ___ walk with

me ___ in the gen - tle rain. ___

Don't ___ be a - fraid; ___ I've a hand ___ for your hand, ___ and I

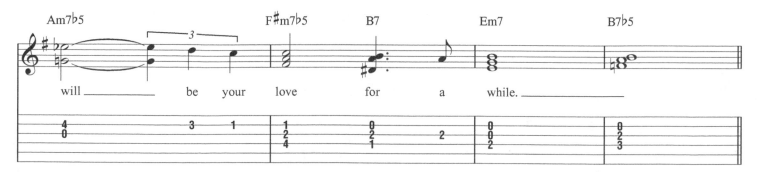

will ___ be your love for a while. ___

Verse

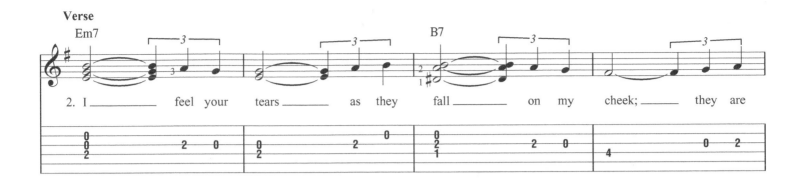

2. I _____ feel your tears _____ as they fall _____ on my cheek; _____ they are

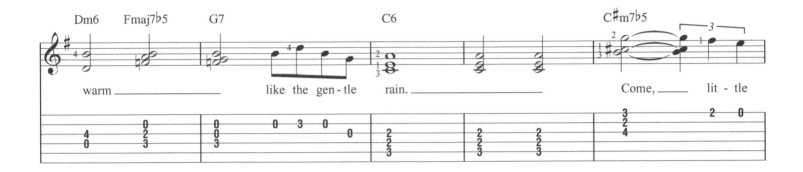

warm _____ like the gen-tle rain. _____ Come, _____ lit-tle

one, _____ you've got me _____ in the world, _____ and our love _____ will be

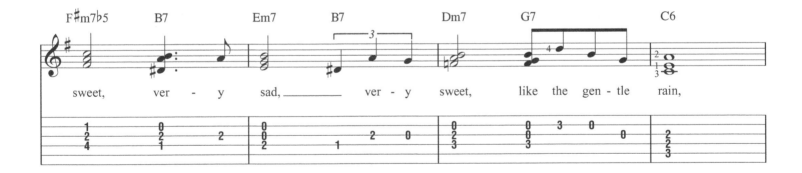

sweet, ver - y sad, _____ ver - y sweet, like the gen - tle rain,

like the gen-tle rain, like the gen-tle rain. _____

Good Bait

By Tadd Dameron and Count Basie

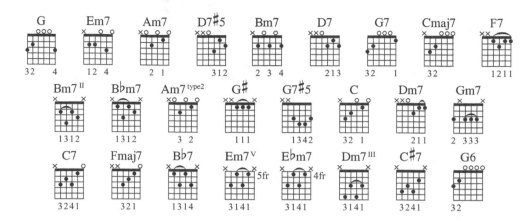

Strum Pattern: 3
Pick Pattern: 3

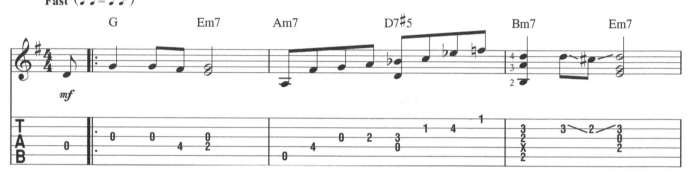

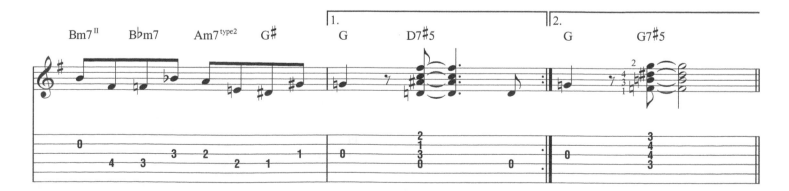

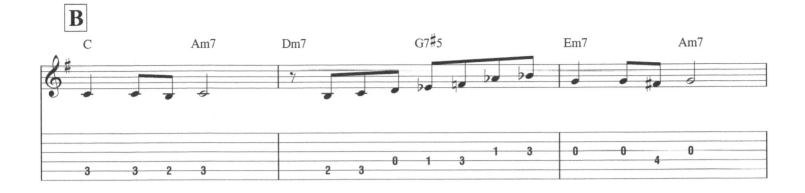

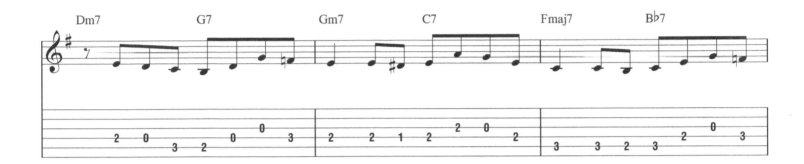

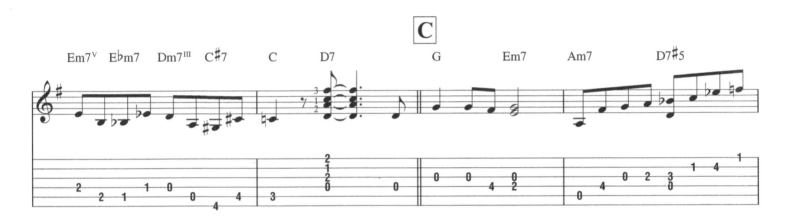

I Get a Kick Out of You

from ANYTHING GOES
Words and Music by Cole Porter

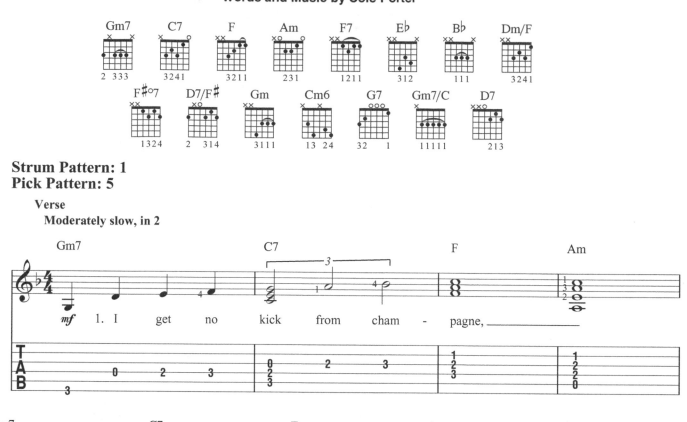

Strum Pattern: 1
Pick Pattern: 5

Verse
Moderately slow, in 2

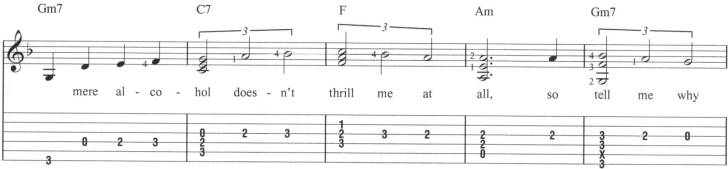

1. I get no kick from cham - pagne,

mere al - co - hol does - n't thrill me at all, so tell me why

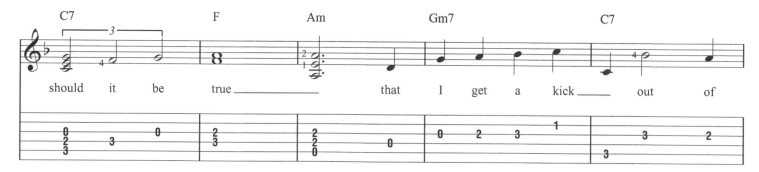

should it be true _____ that I get a kick _____ out of

Verse

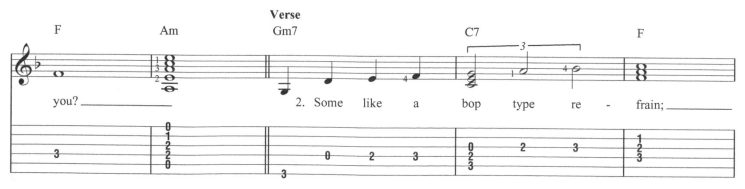

you? _____ 2. Some like a bop type re - frain; _____

I'm sure that if I heard e - ven one

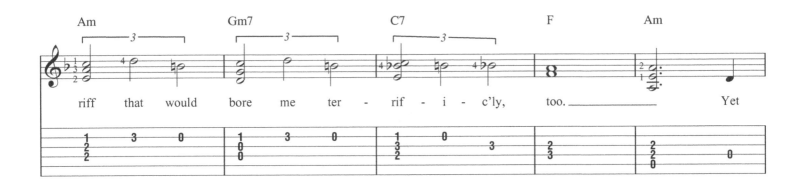

riff that would bore me ter - rif - i - c'ly, too. _____ Yet

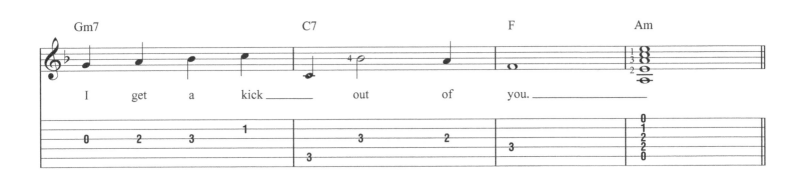

I get a kick _____ out of you. _____

Bridge

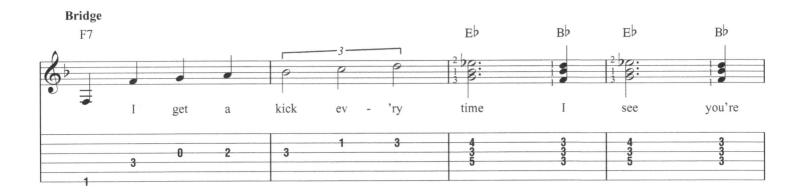

I get a kick ev - 'ry time I see you're

stand - ing there be - fore me. I get a

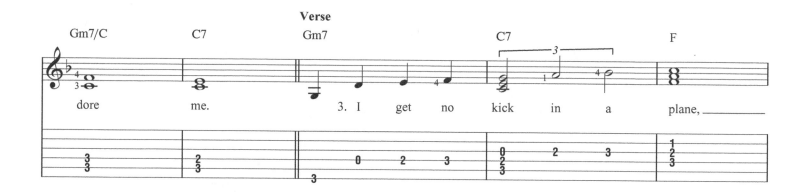

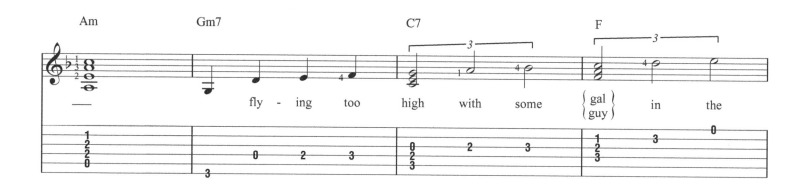

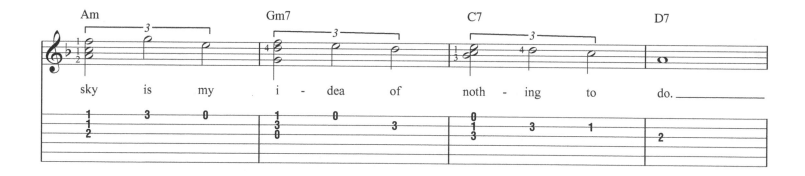

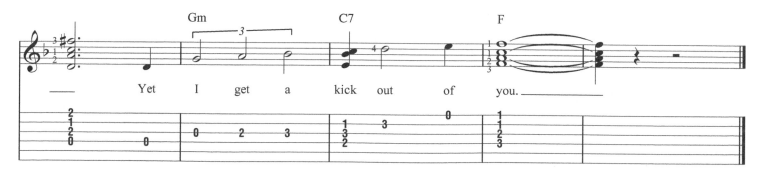

In the Still of the Night

from ROSALIE

Words and Music by Cole Porter

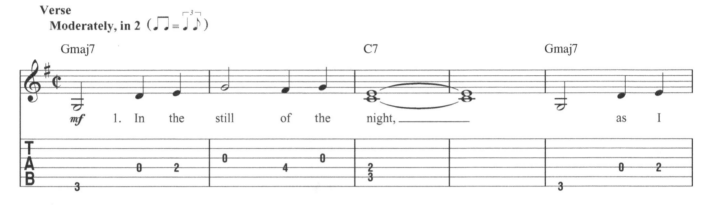

Strum Pattern: 3
Pick Pattern: 3

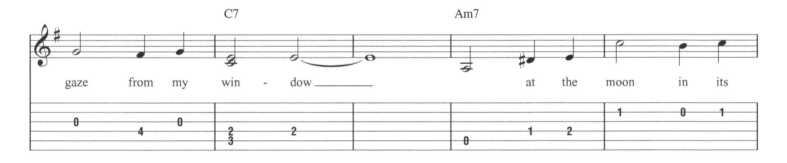

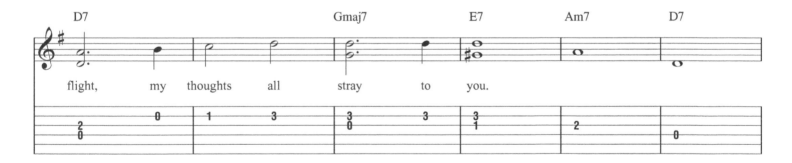

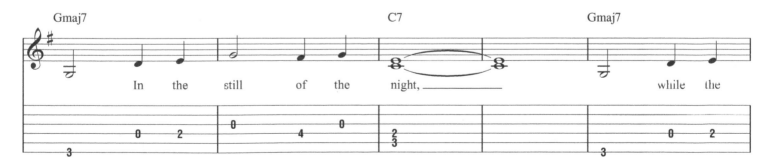

Or will this dream of mine

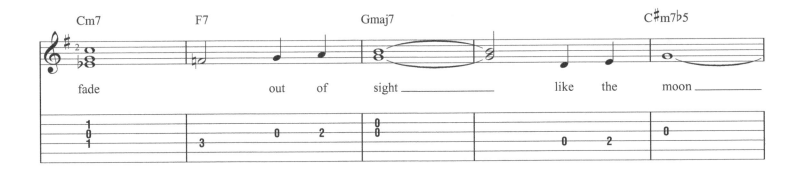

fade out of sight _____ like the moon _____

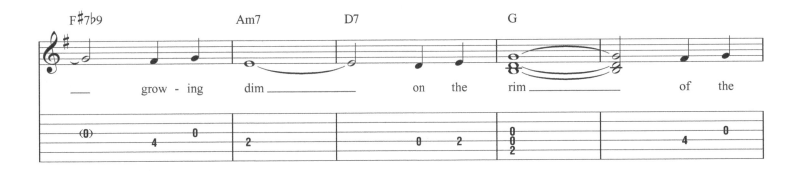

___ grow - ing dim _____ on the rim _____ of the

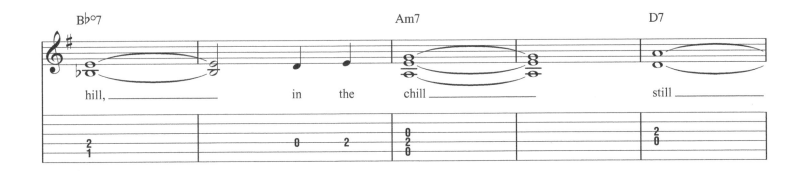

hill, _____ in the chill _____ still _____

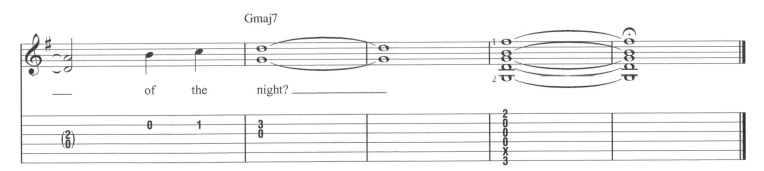

___ of the night? _____

I Got Rhythm

from AN AMERICAN IN PARIS

Music and Lyrics by George Gershwin and Ira Gershwin

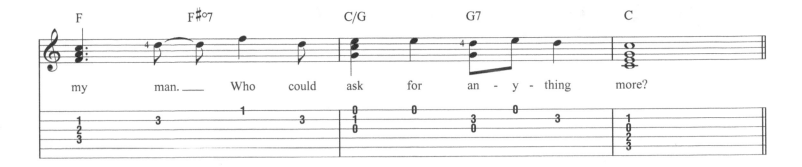

my man.___ Who could ask for an - y - thing more?

Bridge

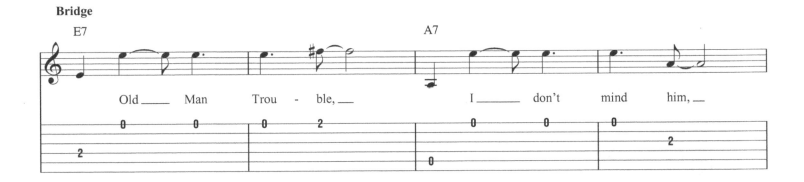

Old___ Man Trou - ble,___ I___ don't mind him, ___

you___ won't find him ___ 'round___ my door.

Verse

3. I_____ got star - light, _ I_____ got sweet dreams, _

I_____ got my man._ Who could ask for an - y - thing more?

I'm Getting Sentimental Over You

Words by Ned Washington
Music by George Bassman

Bridge

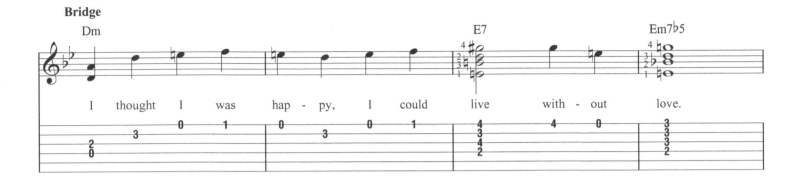

I thought I was hap-py, I could live with-out love.

Now I must ad-mit love is all I'm think-ing of.

Verse

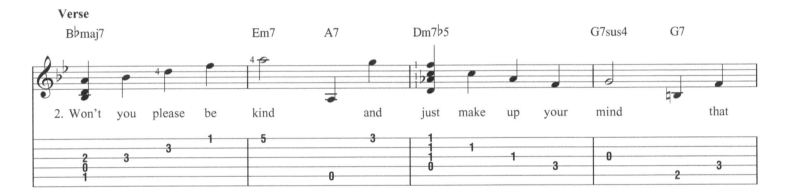

2. Won't you please be kind and just make up your mind that

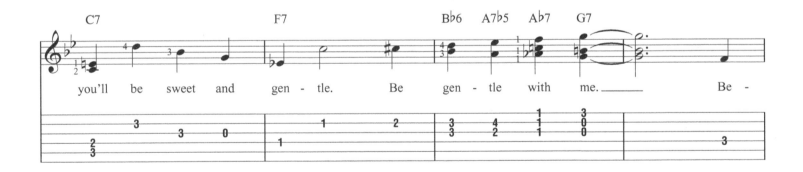

you'll be sweet and gen-tle. Be gen-tle with me._____ Be-

cause I'm sen-ti-men-tal o-ver you._____

I've Grown Accustomed to Her Face

from MY FAIR LADY

Words by Alan Jay Lerner
Music by Frederick Loewe

Strum Pattern: 3
Pick Pattern: 5

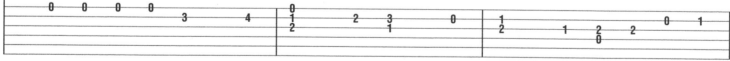

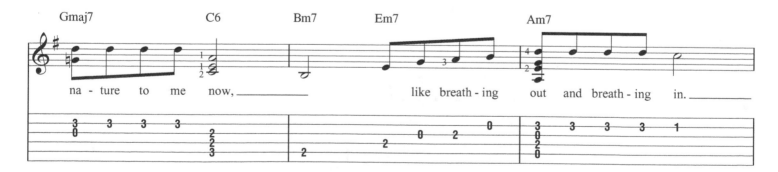

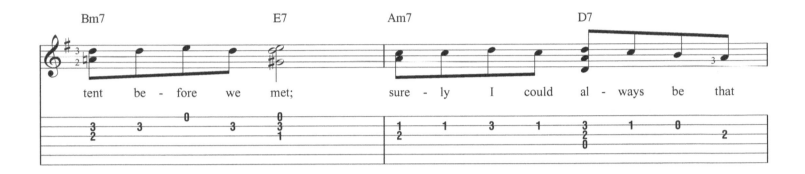

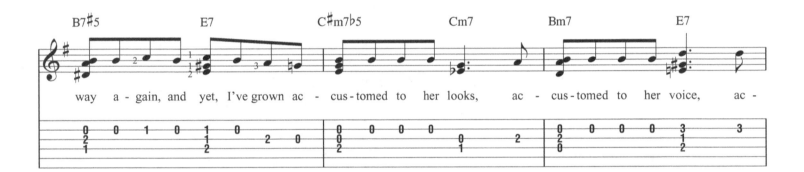

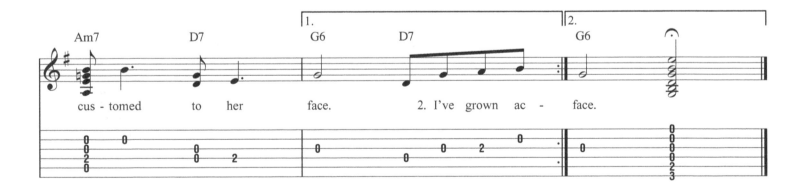

Additional Lyrics

2. I've grown accustomed to her face.
   She makes the day begin.
   I've gotten used to hear her say, "Good morning," ev'ryday.
   Her joys, her woes, her highs, her lows
   Are second nature to me now,
   Like breathing out and breathing in.
   I'm very grateful she's a woman and so easy to forget,
   Rather like a habit one can always break, and yet,
   I've grown accustomed to the trace of something in the air,
   Accustomed to her face.

If I Were a Bell

from GUYS AND DOLLS

By Frank Loesser

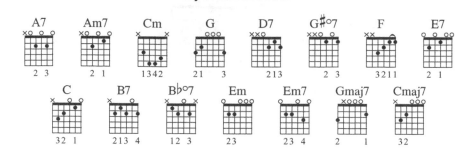

Strum Pattern: 3
Pick Pattern: 3

Verse

Moderately

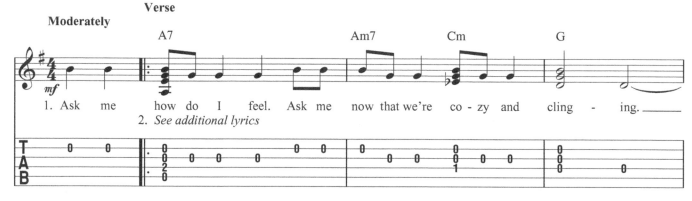

1. Ask me how do I feel. Ask me now that we're co-zy and cling- ing. ____
2. *See additional lyrics*

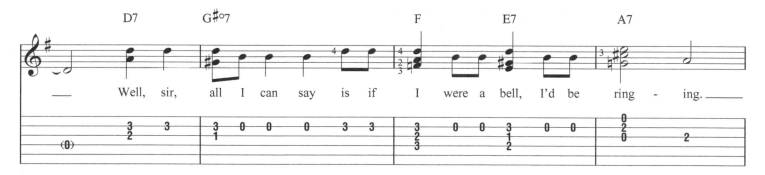

____ Well, sir, all I can say is if I were a bell, I'd be ring- ing. ____

____ From the mo-ment we kissed to - night, that's the way I've just got to be-

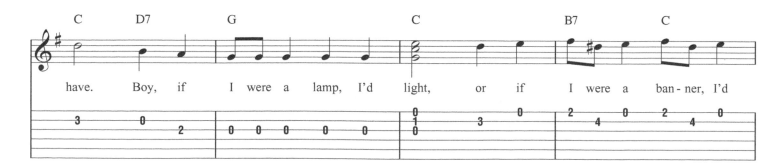

have. Boy, if I were a lamp, I'd light, or if I were a ban-ner, I'd

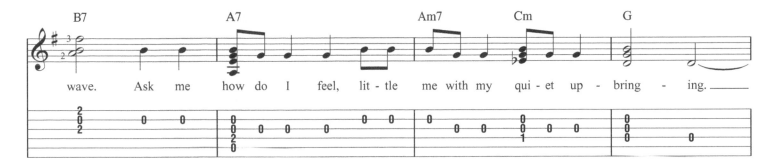

wave. Ask me how do I feel, lit - tle me with my qui - et up - bring - ing. _____

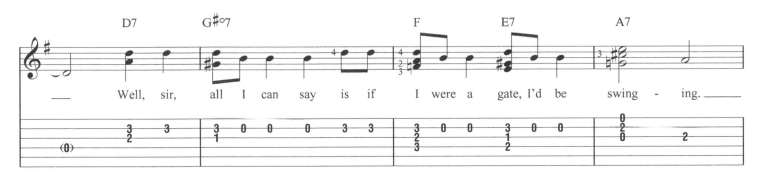

_____ Well, sir, all I can say is if I were a gate, I'd be swing - ing. _____

_____ And if I were a watch, I'd start pop - ping my spring. _____

_____ Or if I were a bell, I'd go ding, dong, ding, dong,

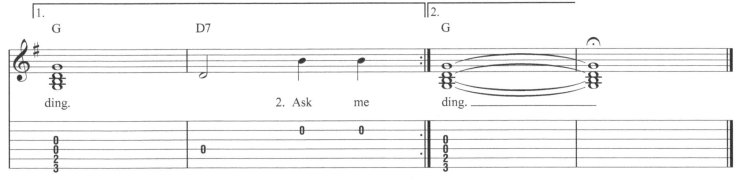

ding.   2. Ask me   ding. _____

Additional Lyrics

2. Ask me how do I feel from this chemistry lesson I'm learning.
Will, sir, all I can say is if I were a bridge, I'd be burning.
Yes, I knew my morale would crack from the wonderful way that you looked.
Boy, if I were a duck, I'd quack, or if I were a goose, I'd be cooked.
Ask me how do I feel, ask me now that we're fondly caressing.
Pal, if I were a salad, I know I'd be splashing my dressing.
Or if I were a season, I'd surely be spring.
Or if I were a bell, I'd go ding, dong, ding, dong, ding.

In Your Own Sweet Way

By Dave Brubeck

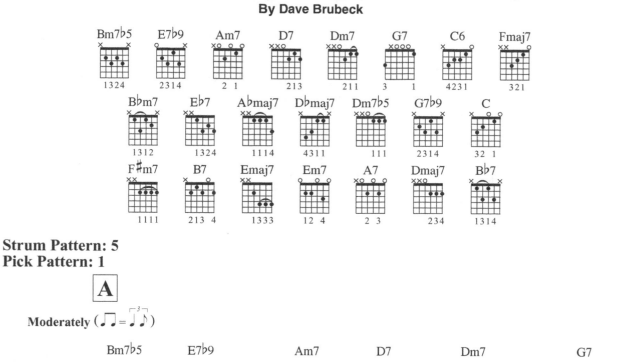

Strum Pattern: 5
Pick Pattern: 1

A

Moderately

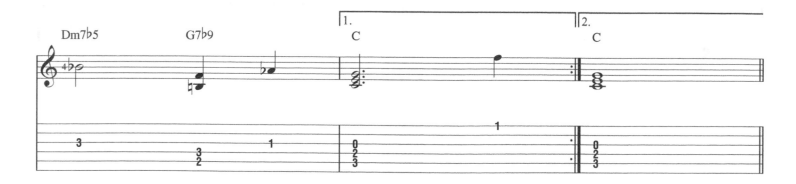

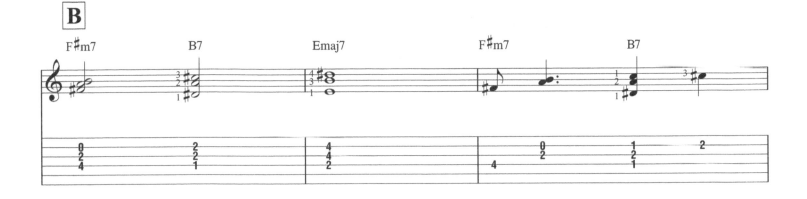

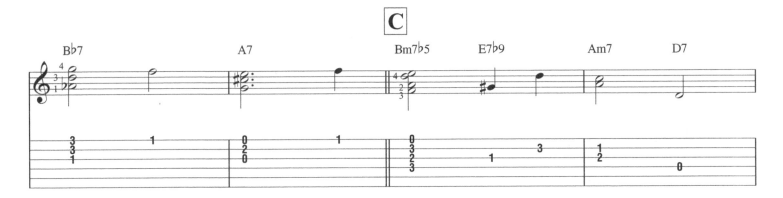

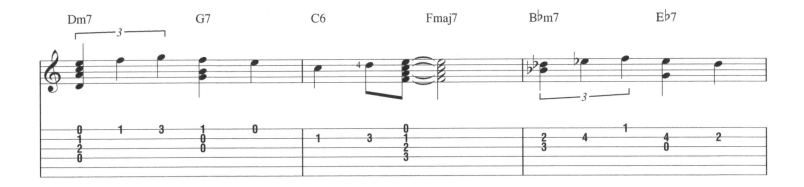

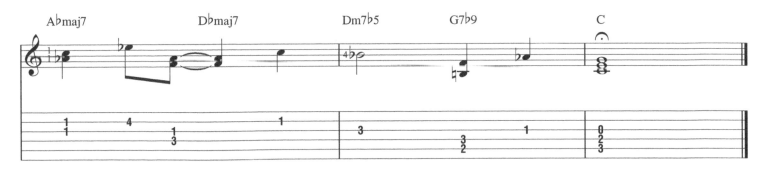

It Ain't Necessarily So

from PORGY AND BESS

Music and Lyrics by George Gershwin, DuBose and Dorothy Heyward and Ira Gershwin

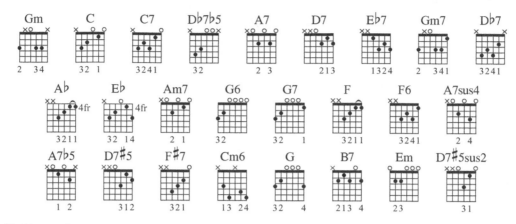

Strum Pattern: 3
Pick Pattern: 3

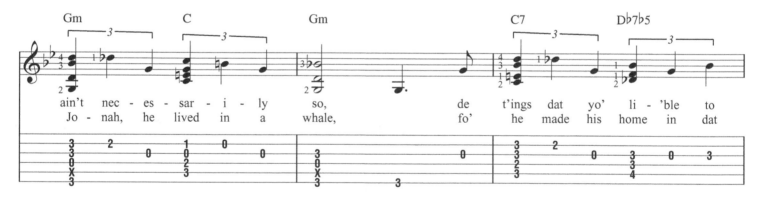

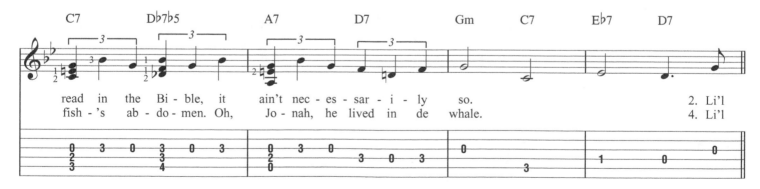

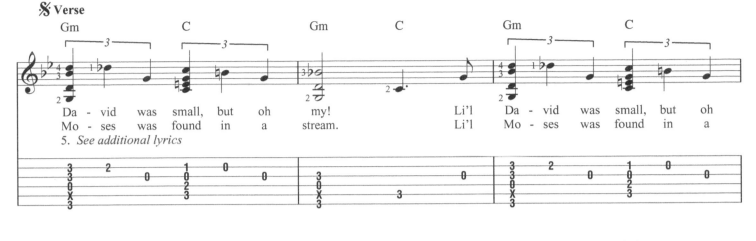

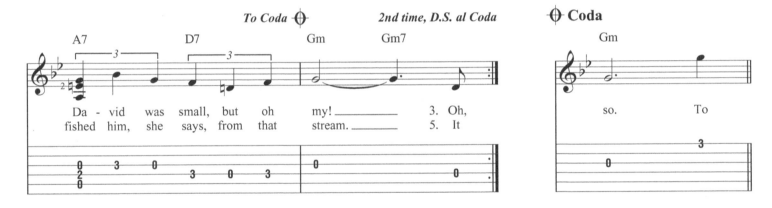

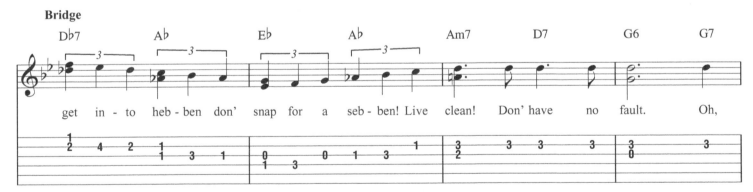

Bridge

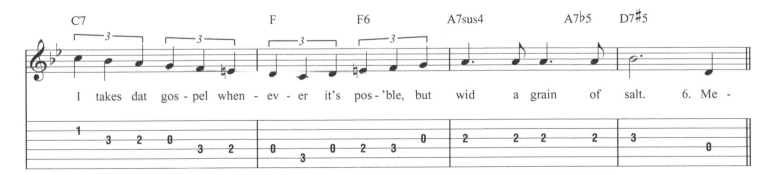

Verse

Additional Lyrics

5. It ain't necessarily so, it ain't necessarily so.
   Dey tell all you chillun de debble's a villun,
   But 'taint necessarily so.

Like Young

Words and Music by Paul Webster and Andre Previn

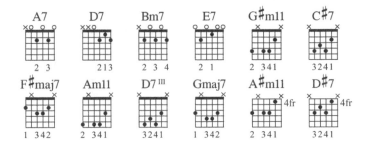

Strum Pattern: 3
Pick Pattern: 3

Verse
Moderately

1. I'm out do-in' the u-su-al plac - es, and I'm liv-in' it
2. *See additional lyrics*

like ____ young. ____ Then I dig me this face of all fac - es,

{she's / he's} the cra - zi - est like ____ young. ____ {She / He} drinks cof - fee at

Ca - fe Es - pres - so. {She/He} reads Ker - ou - ac like ____ young. __

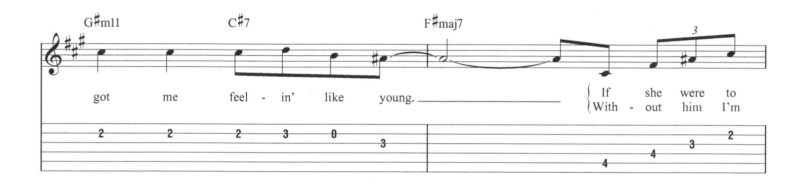

like ____ wow! __ I'm ____ all un - strung, ____ 'cause, man, {she's/he's}

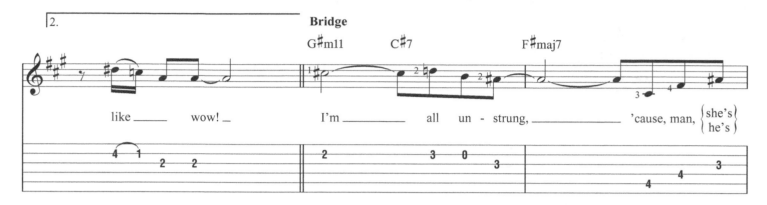

got me feel - in' like young. ____ {If she were to / With - out him I'm}

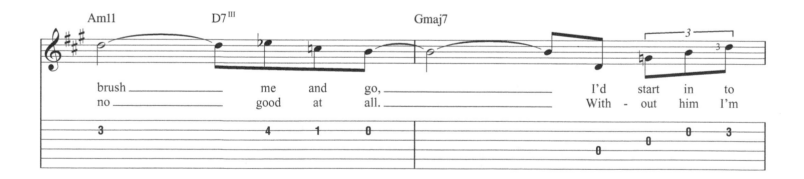

brush ____ me and go, ____ I'd start in to
no ____ good at all. ____ With - out him I'm

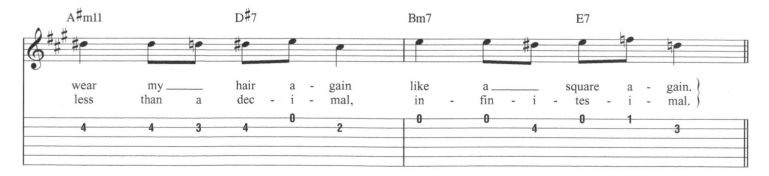

wear my ____ hair a - gain like a ____ square a - gain. }
less than a dec - i - mal, in - fin - i - tes - i - mal. }

Verse

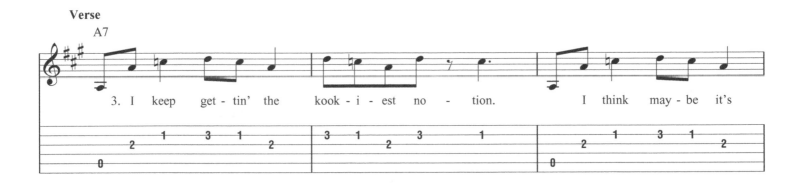

3. I keep get - tin' the kook - i - est no - tion. I think may - be it's

like ___ love. ___ I been feel - in' a cra - zy e - mo - tion.

I think, ba - by, it's like ___ love. ___ Now we're rid - in' a

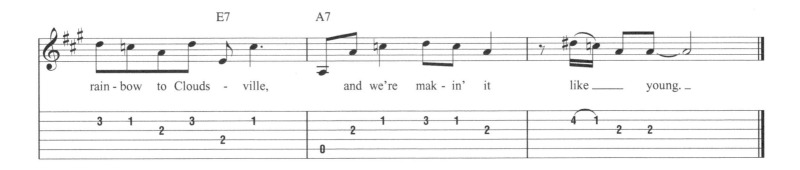

rain - bow to Clouds - ville, and we're mak - in' it like ___ young. ___

Additional Lyrics

2. { She / He } goes where all the angry young men go,
Recites poetry like young.
We start blowin' the pad around 'leven,
And we're homin' it like now.
We spin records on cloud number seven,
And { she's / he's } reachin' me like wow!

Just Friends

Lyrics by Sam M. Lewis
Music by John Klenner

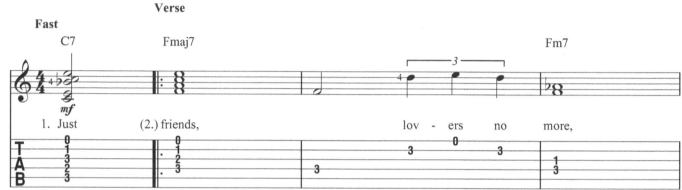

Strum Pattern: 5
Pick Pattern: 1

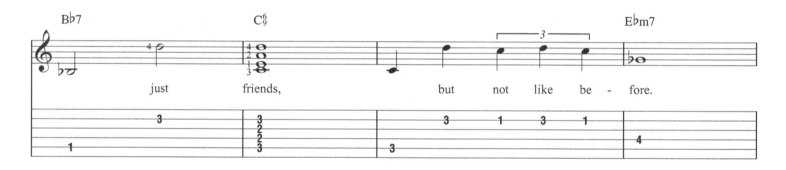

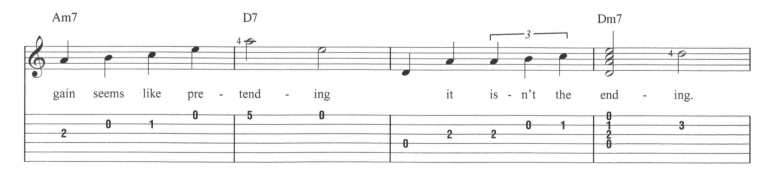

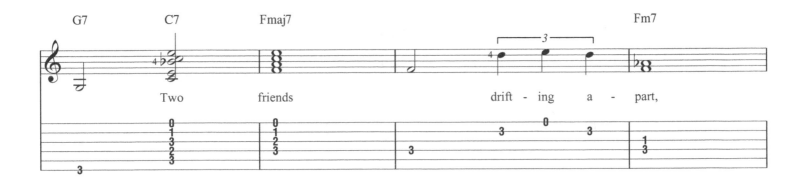

Two   friends   drift - ing a - part,

two   friends   but one bro - ken heart.

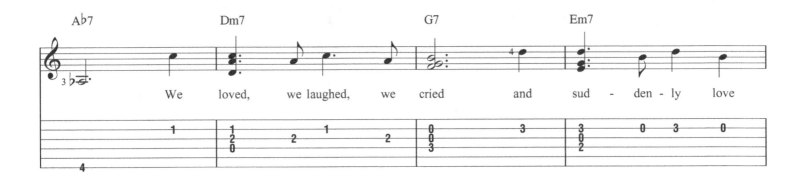

We loved,   we laughed,   we cried   and   sud - den - ly love

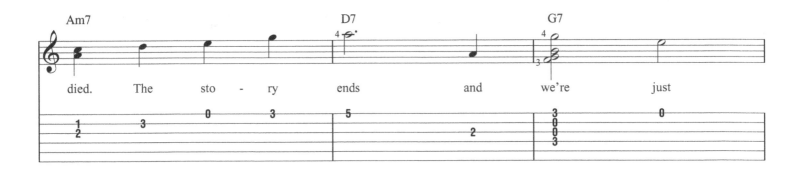

died.   The sto - ry   ends   and   we're   just

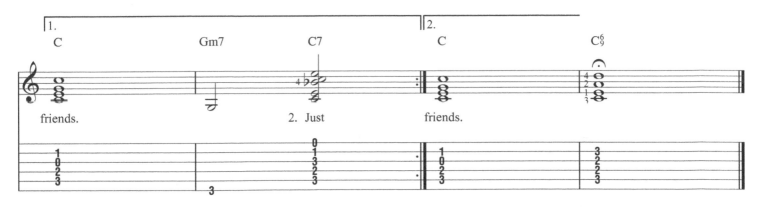

friends.   2. Just   friends.

Laura

Lyrics by Johnny Mercer
Music by David Raksin

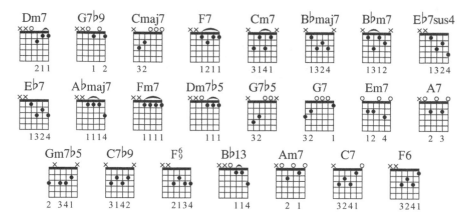

Strum Pattern: 3
Pick Pattern: 3

Verse
Slow

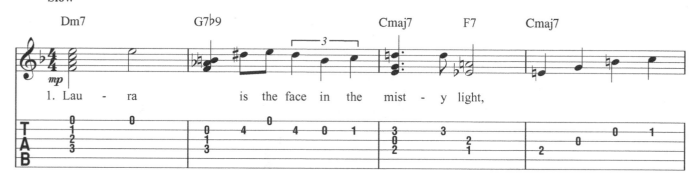

1. Lau - ra   is the face in the mist - y light,

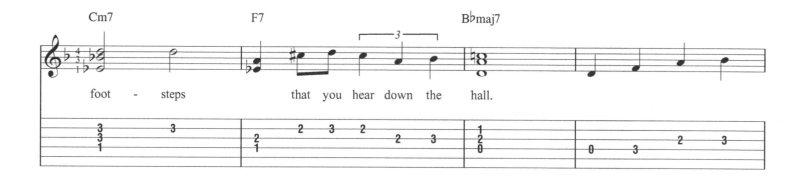

foot - steps   that you hear down the   hall.

The   laugh   that floats on a   sum - mer night   that you   can

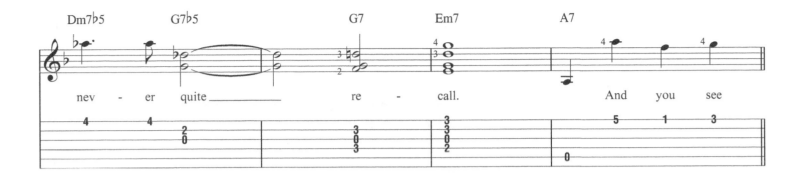

never quite ____ re - call. And you see

Verse

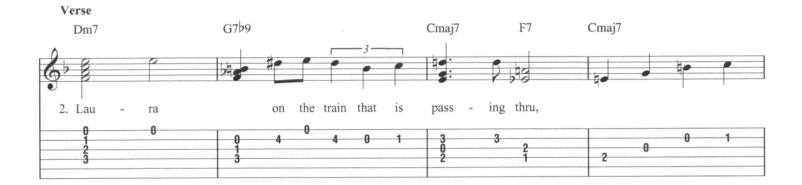

2. Lau - ra on the train that is pass - ing thru,

those eyes how fa - mil - iar they seem.

She gave your ver - y first kiss to you. That was

Lau - ra but she's on - ly a dream. ____

Li'l Darlin'

By Neal Hefti

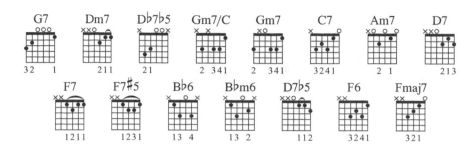

Strum Pattern: 4
Pick Pattern: 3

Moderately slow

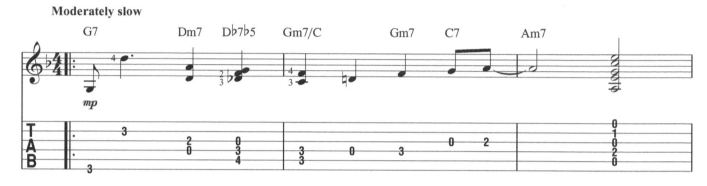

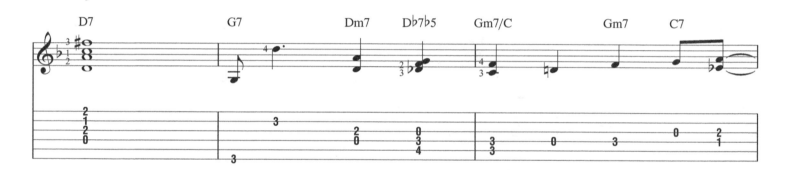

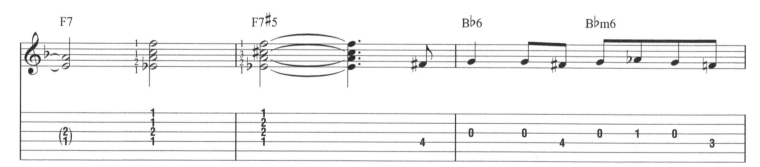

3rd time, To Coda ⊕

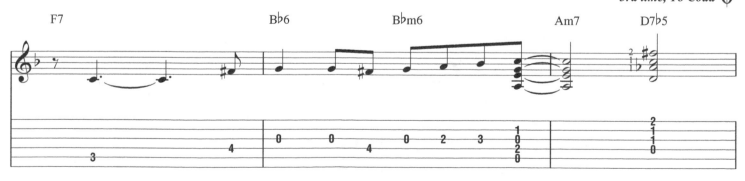

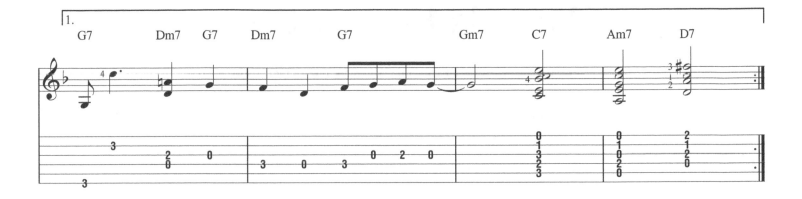

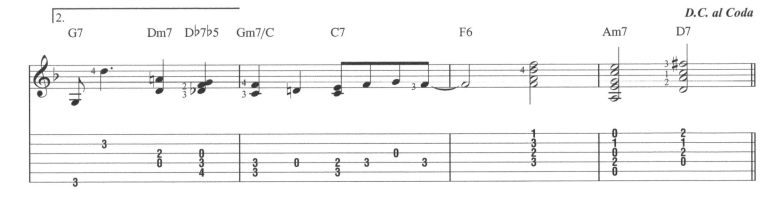

D.C. al Coda

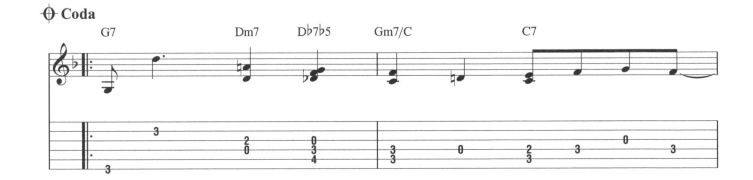

⊕ Coda

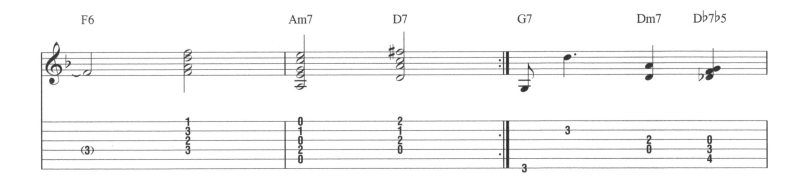

Love Is Here to Stay

from GOLDWYN FOLLIES

Music and Lyrics by George Gershwin and Ira Gershwin

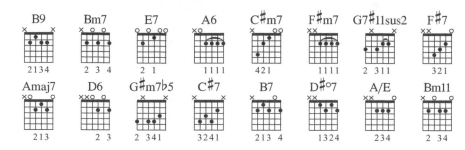

Strum Pattern: 3
Pick Pattern: 3

Verse
Moderately fast

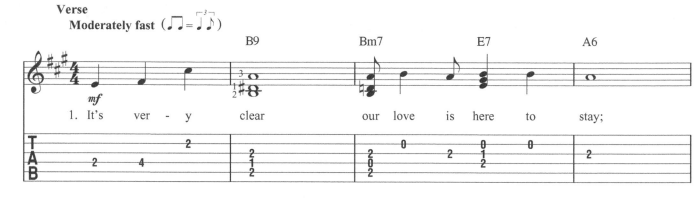

1. It's ver-y clear our love is here to stay;

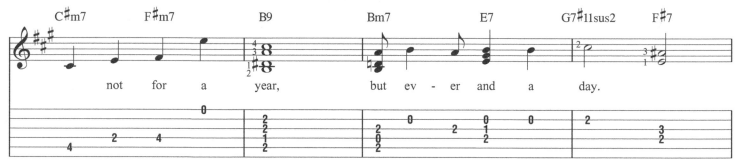

not for a year, but ev-er and a day.

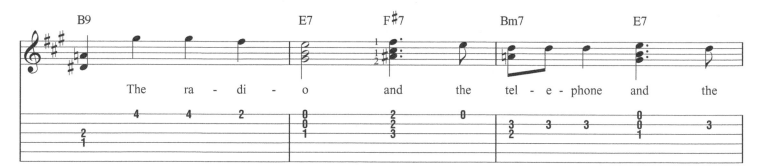

The ra-di-o and the tel-e-phone and the

mov-ies that we know may just be pass-ing fan-cies,

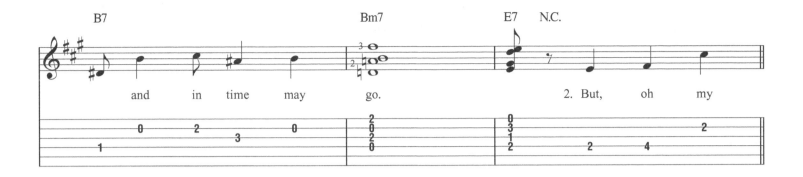

Verse

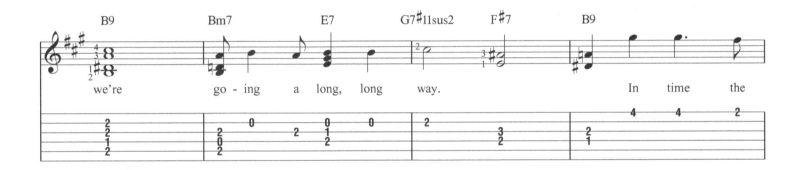

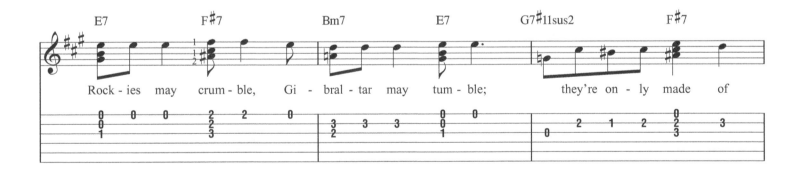

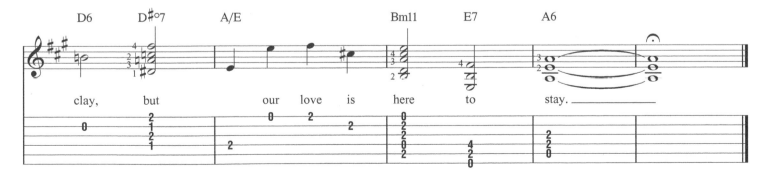

Mack the Knife

from THE THREEPENNY OPERA

English Words by Marc Blitzstein
Original German Words by Bert Brecht
Music by Kurt Weill

*Capo III

Strum Pattern: 3
Pick Pattern: 3

*Optional: To match recording, place capo at 3rd fret.

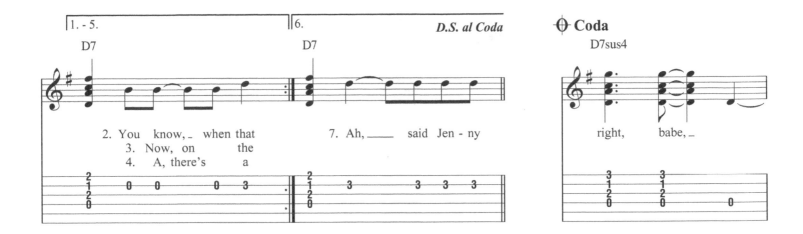

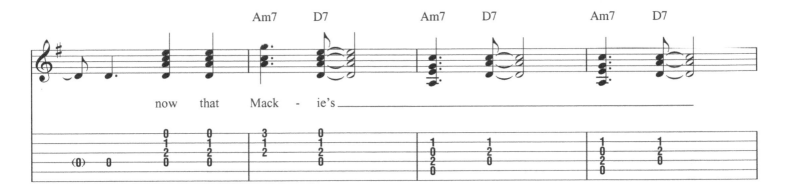

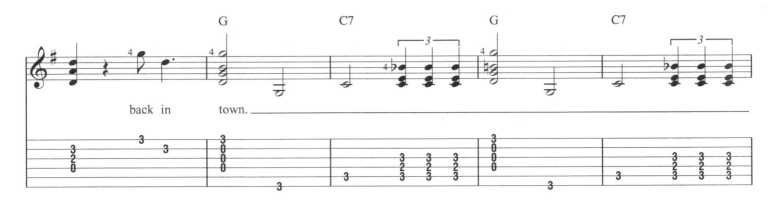

Additional Lyrics

4. A, there's a tugboat down by the river, don't ya know,
   Where a cement bag's just a droopin' on down.
   Whoa, that cement is just, it's there for the weight, dear,
   Five'll get ya ten ol' Mackie's back in town.

5. Now'd you hear 'bout Louie Miller? He disappeared, babe,
   After drawin' out all his hard-earned cash.
   And now Mackheath spends just like a sailor.
   Could it be our boy's done somethin' rash?

6. Now, Jenny Diver, yeah, Sukey Tawdry,
   Oo, Miss Lotte Lenya, and Lucy Brown;
   Oh, the line forms on the right, babe,
   Now that Mackie's back in town.

7. Ah, said Jenny Diver, whoa, Sukey Tawdry,
   Look out a Miss Lotte Lenya and ol' Lucy Brown;
   Yes, that line forms on the right, babe,
   Now that Mackie's back in town.
Spoken: Look out, ol' Mackie is back!

Makin' Whoopee!

from WHOOPEE!

Lyrics by Gus Kahn
Music by Walter Donaldson

love - nest,   down where the ros - es cling;

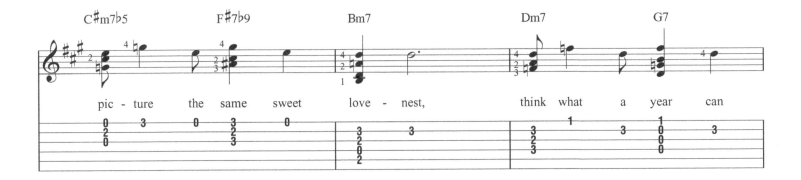

pic - ture the same sweet love - nest,   think what a year can

Verse

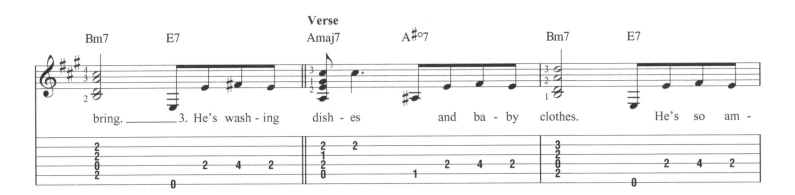

bring. _____ 3. He's wash - ing dish - es   and ba - by clothes.   He's so am -

bi - tious; he e - ven sews.   But don't for - get, folks,   that's what you

get, folks,   for mak - in' whoop - ee! _____

Night and Day

from GAY DIVORCE
Words and Music by Cole Porter

Strum Pattern: 5
Pick Pattern: 1

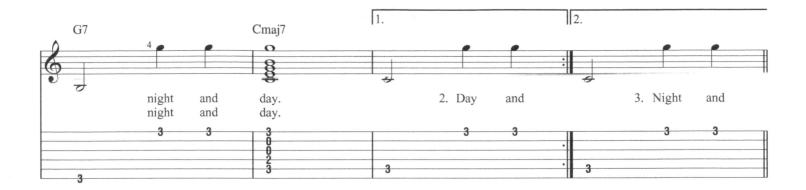

Verse

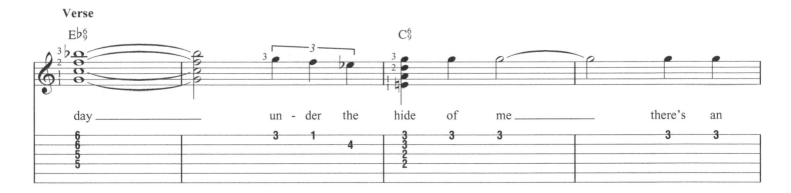

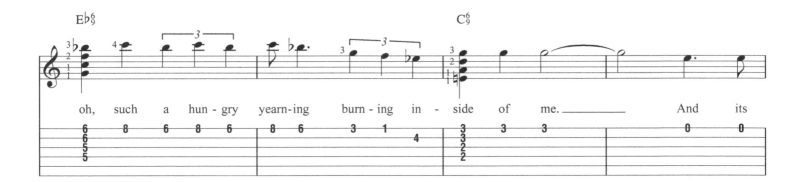

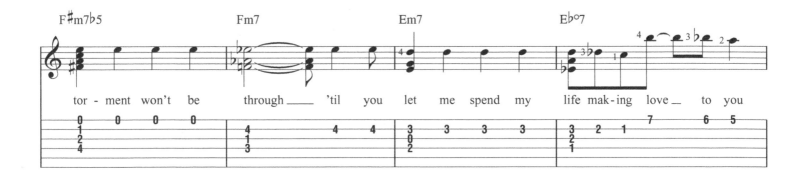

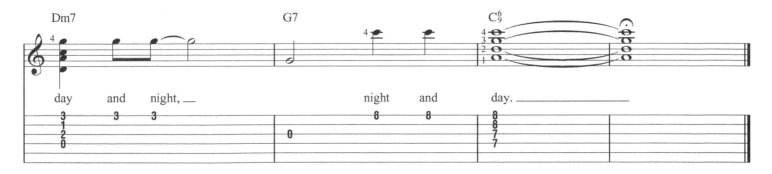

Oh, Lady Be Good!

from LADY, BE GOOD!

Music and Lyrics by George Gershwin and Ira Gershwin

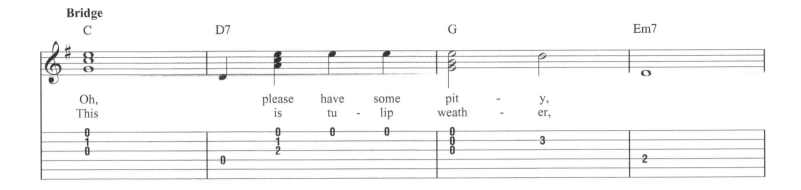

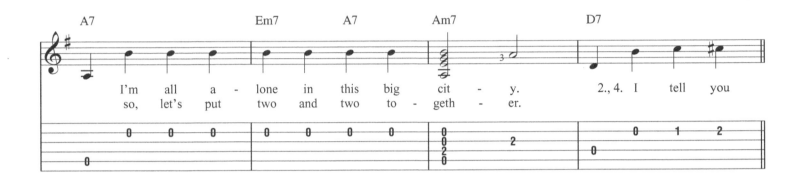

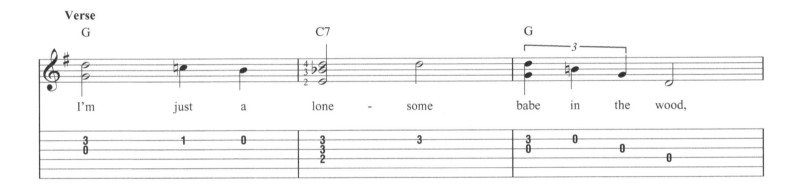

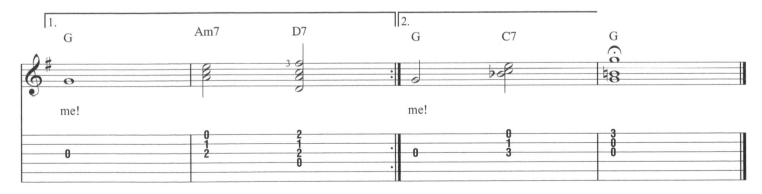

One O'Clock Jump

By Count Basie

Strum Pattern: 3
Pick Pattern: 3

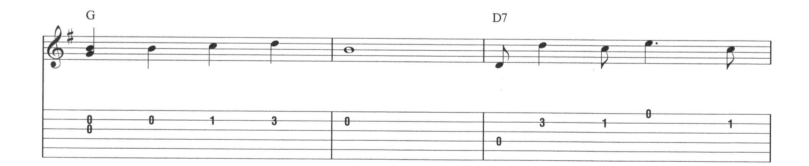

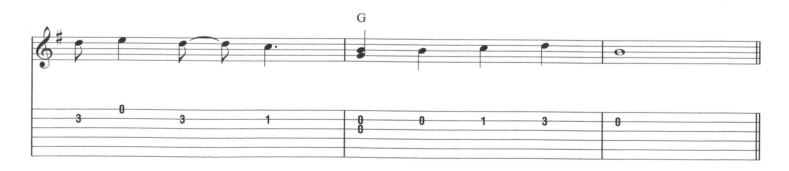

B

Over the Rainbow

from THE WIZARD OF OZ

Music by Harold Arlen
Lyric by E.Y. "Yip" Harburg

Strum Pattern: 3
Pick Pattern: 3

Bridge

day I'll wish up-on a star and wake up where the clouds are far be - hind me,

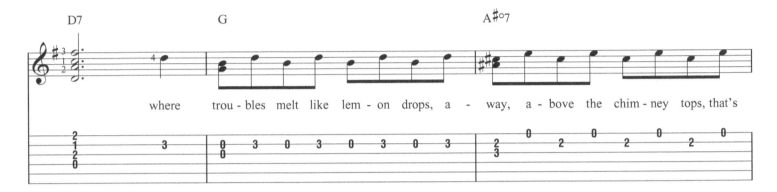

where trou - bles melt like lem - on drops, a - way, a - bove the chim - ney tops, that's

Verse

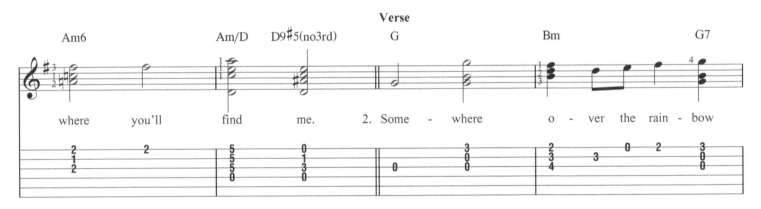

where you'll find me. 2. Some - where o - ver the rain - bow

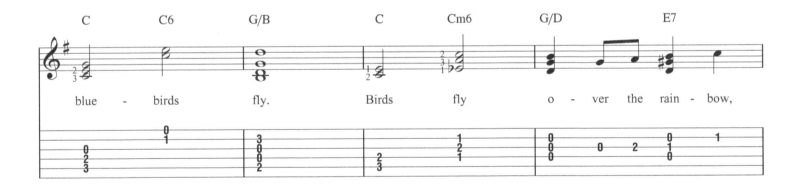

blue - birds fly. Birds fly o - ver the rain - bow,

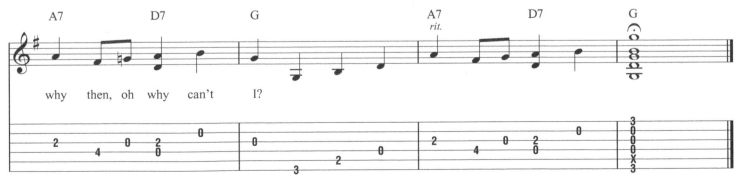

why then, oh why can't I?

Rosetta

Words and Music by Earl Hines and Henri Wood

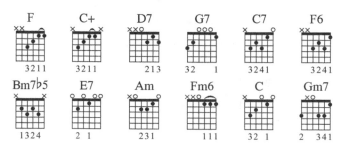

Strum Pattern: 3
Pick Pattern: 3

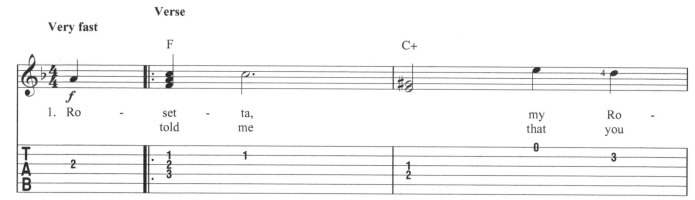

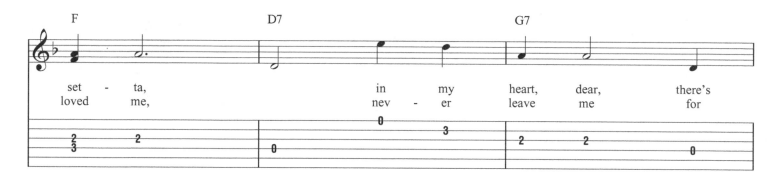

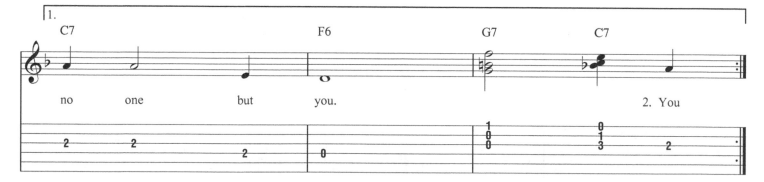

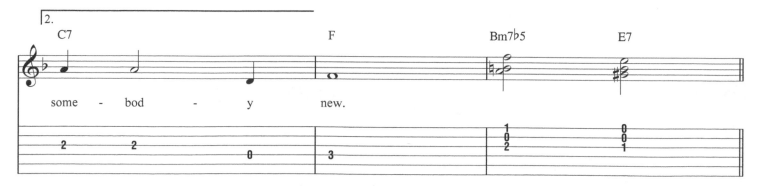

Bridge

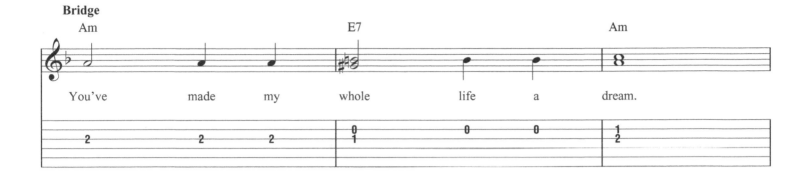

You've made my whole life a dream.

I pray you'll make it come

Verse

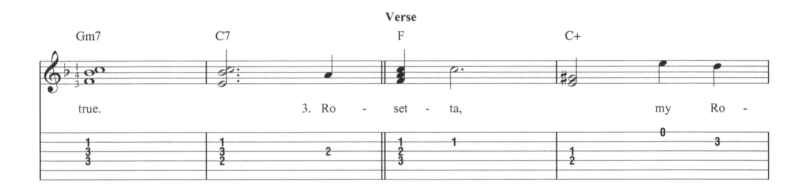

true. 3. Ro - set - ta, my Ro -

set - ta, please say I'm just the

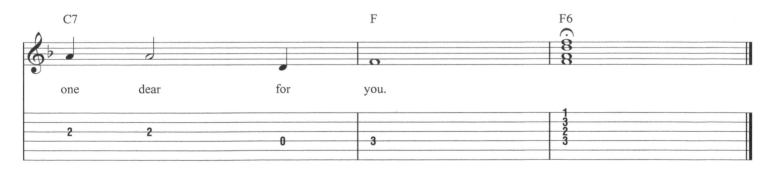

one dear for you.

'S Wonderful

from FUNNY FACE

Music and Lyrics by George Gershwin and Ira Gershwin

Strum Pattern: 3
Pick Pattern: 3

Verse
Moderately, in 2

88

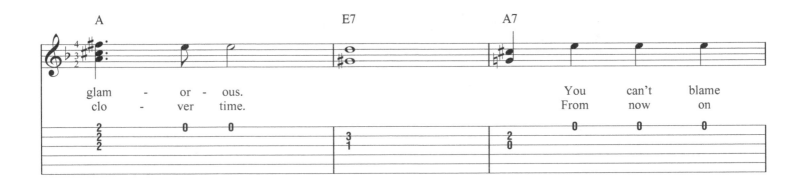

glam - or - ous.
clo - ver time.
You can't blame
From now on

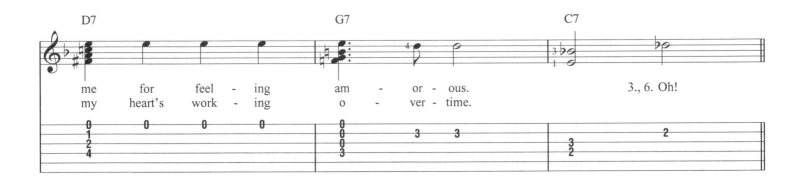

me for feel - ing am - or - ous.
my heart's work - ing o - ver - time.
3., 6. Oh!

Verse

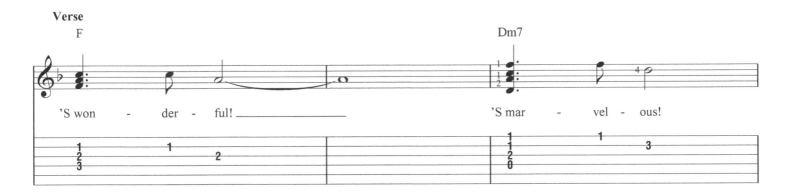

'S won - der - ful! _____
'S mar - vel - ous!

To Coda ⊕

That you should care for

D.C. al Coda
(take repeat)

⊕ **Coda**

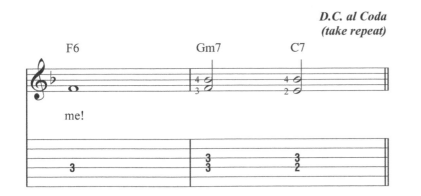

me!

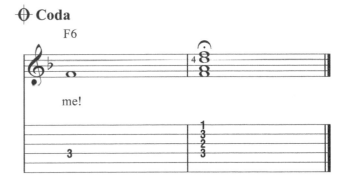

me!

September in the Rain

Words by Al Dubin
Music by Harry Warren

G6 Dm7 G7 C6 F7 Am7 D7 Em7 A7

Strum Pattern: 3
Pick Pattern: 3

Verse
Moderately

1. The leaves of brown came tum - bling down, re - ing
   sun went out just like a dy - ing

mem - ber? _____ In Sep - tem - ber, _____
em - ber, _____ that Sep - tem - ber _____

in the rain. _____ 2. The
in the

rain. _____ To ev - 'ry word of

Bridge

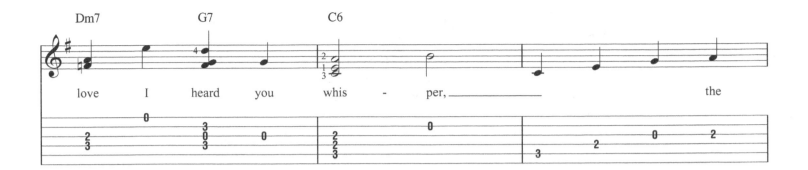

love I heard you whis - per, _____ the

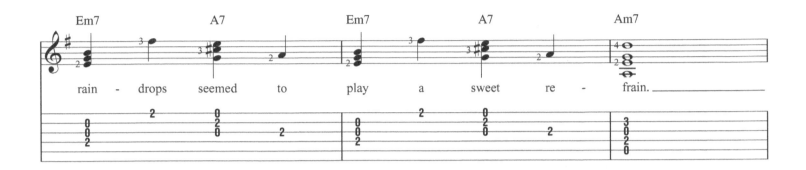

rain - drops seemed to play a sweet re - frain. _____

Outro-Verse

___ 3. Though spring is here, to me it's still Sep -

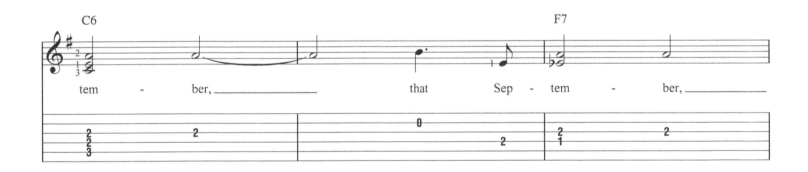

tem - ber, _____ that Sep - tem - ber, _____

___ in the rain. _____

The Shadow of Your Smile

Love Theme from THE SANDPIPER

Music by Johnny Mandel
Words by Paul Francis Webster

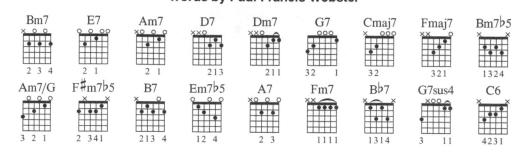

Strum Pattern: 2
Pick Pattern: 2

Verse
Moderately slow

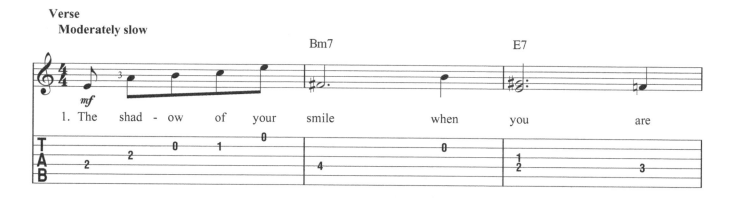

1. The shad-ow of your smile when you are

gone will col-or all my dreams and

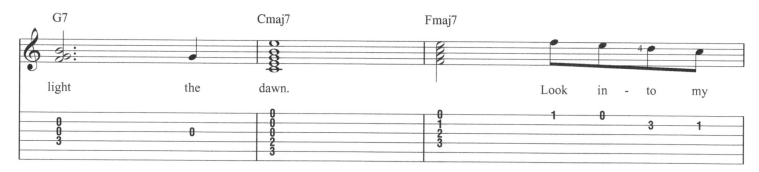

light the dawn. Look in-to my

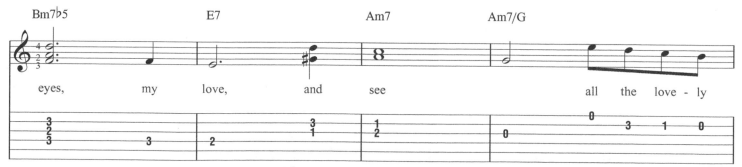

eyes, my love, and see all the love-ly

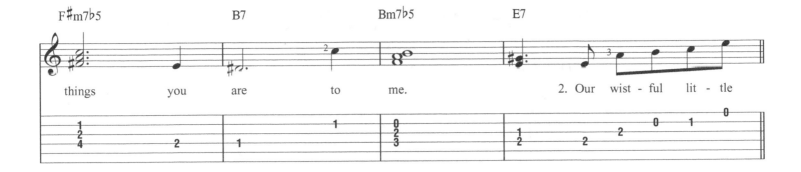

things you are to me. 2. Our wist - ful lit - tle

Verse

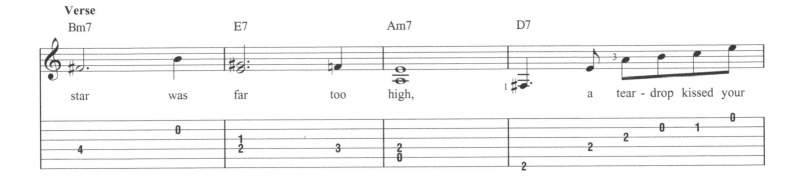

star was far too high, a tear - drop kissed your

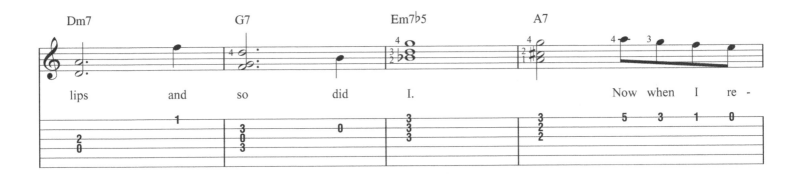

lips and so did I. Now when I re -

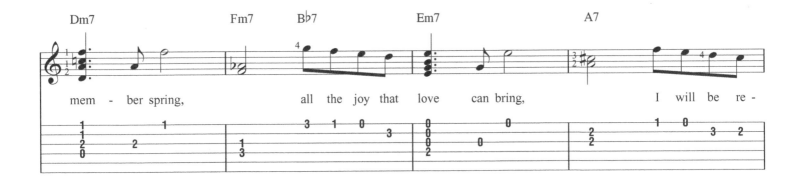

mem - ber spring, all the joy that love can bring, I will be re -

mem - ber - ing the shad - ow of your smile. _____

Someone to Watch Over Me

from OH, KAY!

Music and Lyrics by George Gershwin and Ira Gershwin

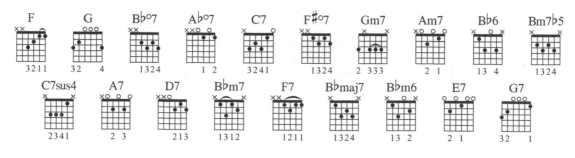

Strum Pattern: 3
Pick Pattern: 3

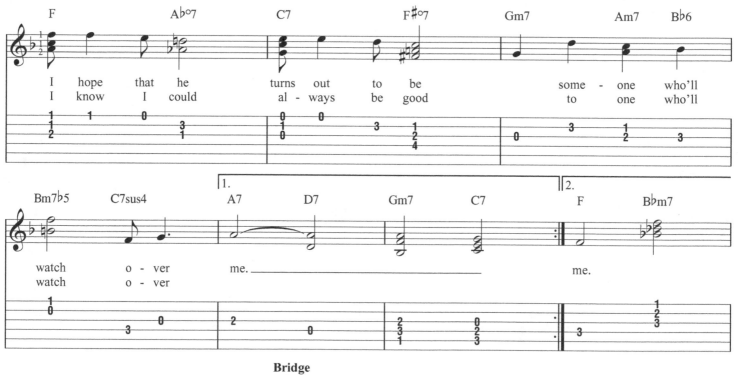

1. There's a some-bod-y I'm long-ing to see.
2. I'm a lit-tle lamb who's lost in the wood.

I hope that he turns out to be some-one who'll
I know I could al-ways be good to one who'll

watch o-ver me.
watch o-ver

me.

Bridge

Al-though he may not be the man some girls

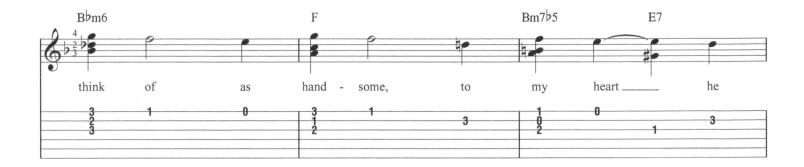

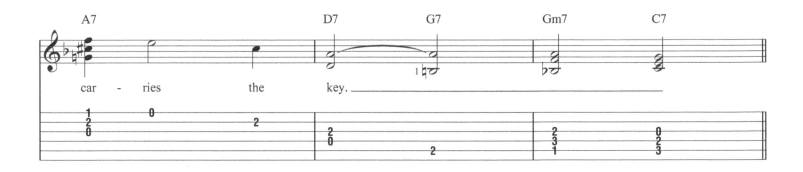

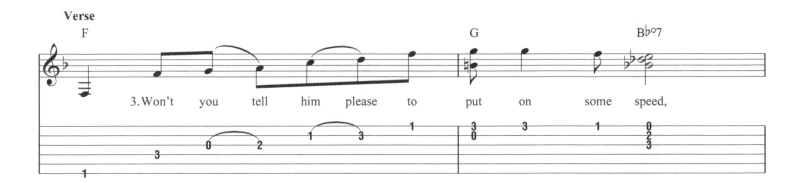

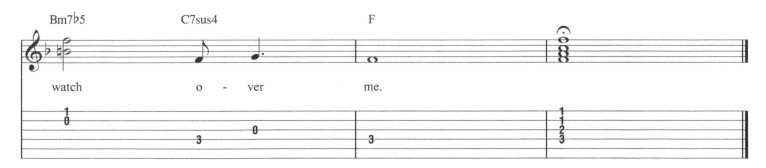

Spring Is Here

from I MARRIED AN ANGEL

Words by Lorenz Hart
Music by Richard Rodgers

Strum Pattern: 3
Pick Pattern: 3

Verse
Moderately slow, in 2

Verse

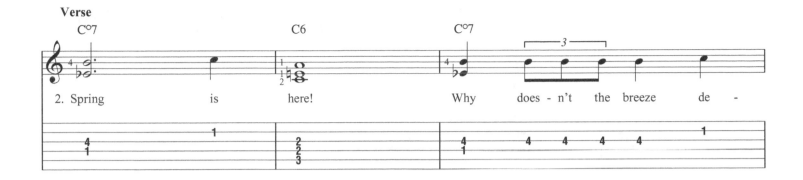

2. Spring is here! Why does-n't the breeze de -

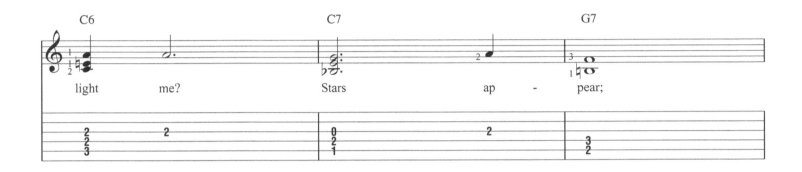

light me? Stars ap - pear;

why does-n't the night in - vite me? May - be it's be -

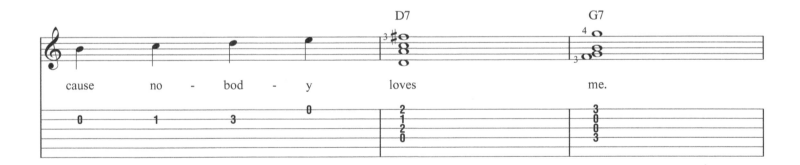

cause no - bod - y loves me.

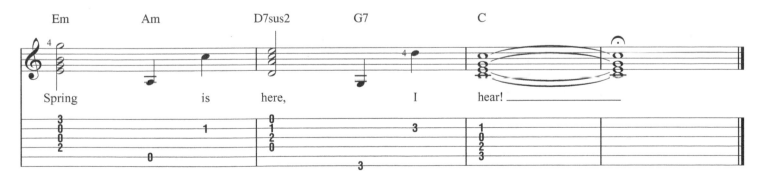

Spring is here, I hear!

Star Eyes

Words by Don Raye
Music by Gene DePaul

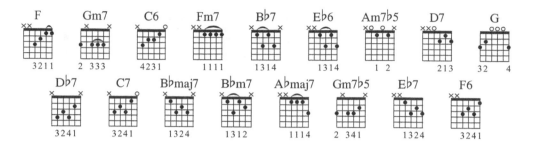

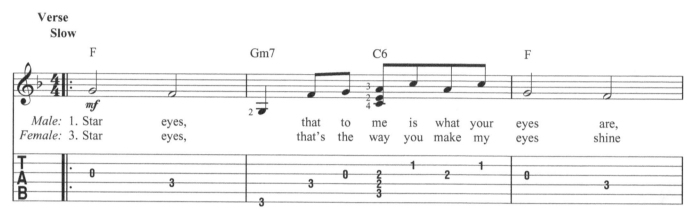

Strum Pattern: 2
Pick Pattern: 2

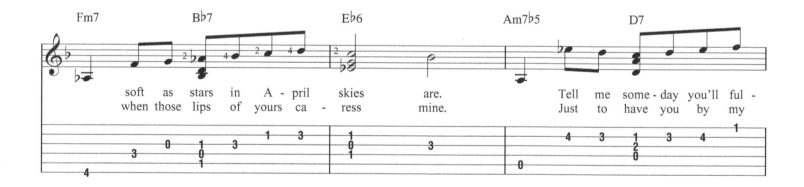

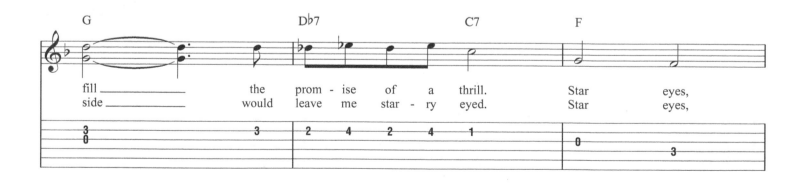

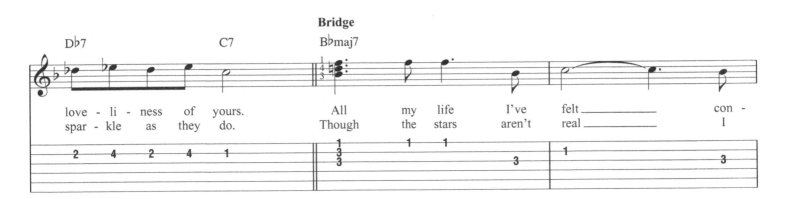

Bridge

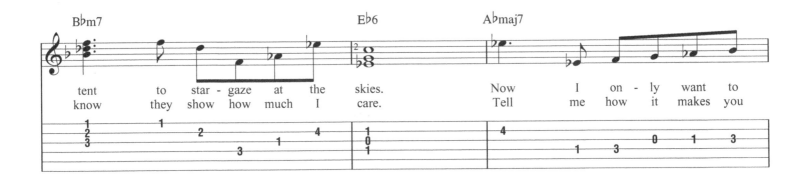

Verse

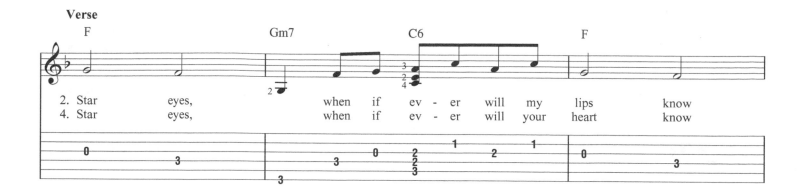

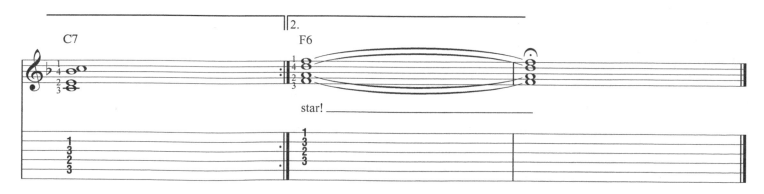

Summer Wind

English Words by Johnny Mercer
Original German Lyrics by Hans Bradtke
Music by Henry Mayer

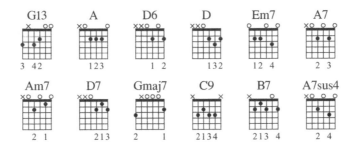

Strum Pattern: 4
Pick Pattern: 4

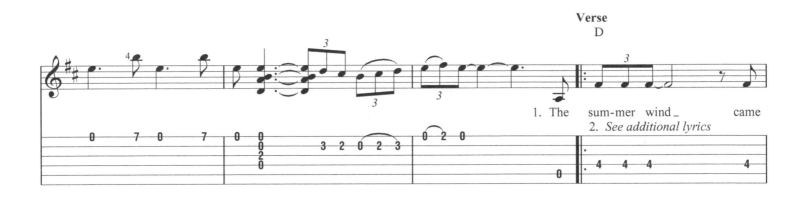

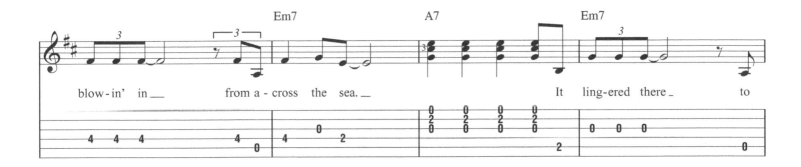

touch your hair __ and walk with me. __ All sum-mer long __ we

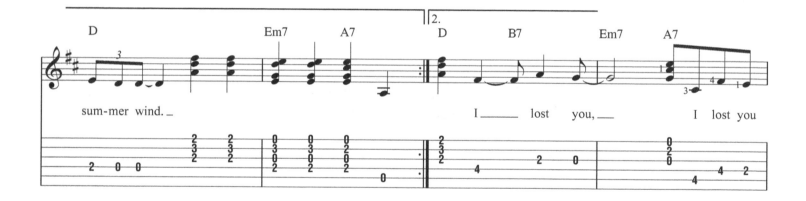

sang a song, __ and then we strolled that gold-en sand, two sweet-hearts _____ and the

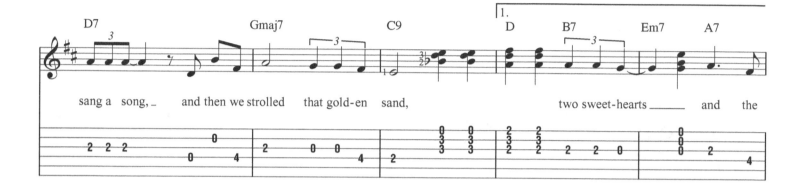

sum-mer wind. __ I _____ lost you, __ I lost you

Verse

to the sum-mer wind. 3. The au-tumn wind _ and the win-ter winds, _ they have

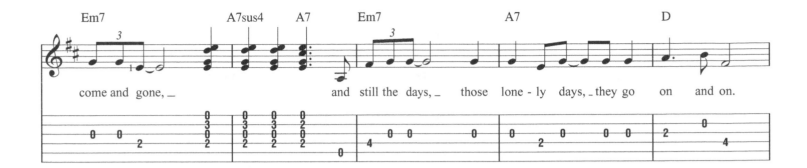

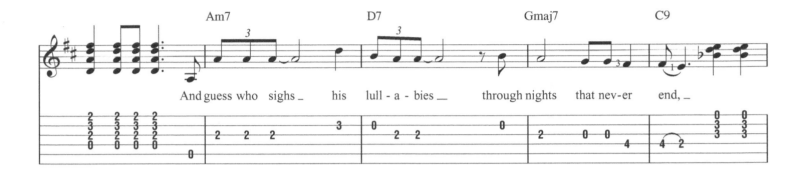

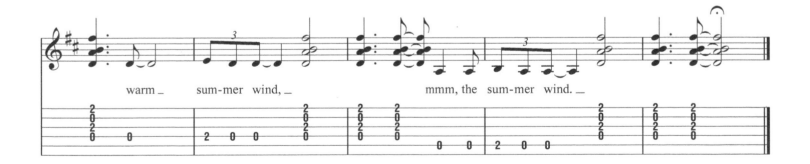

Additional Lyrics

2. Like painted kites, those days and nights, they went flyin' by.
The world was new beneath the blue umbrella sky.
Then softer than a piper man, one day it called to you.
I lost you, I lost you to the summer wind.

Summertime

from PORGY AND BESS®

Music and Lyrics by George Gershwin, DuBose and Dorothy Heyward and Ira Gershwin

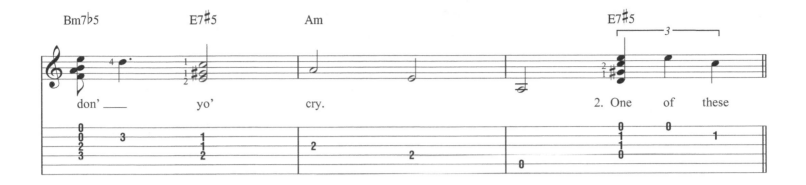

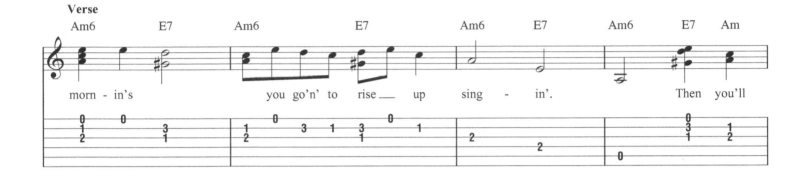

Verse

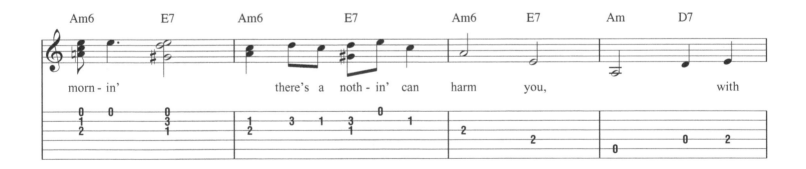

The Surrey with the Fringe on Top

from OKLAHOMA!

Lyrics by Oscar Hammerstein II
Music by Richard Rodgers

Strum Pattern: 3
Pick Pattern: 3

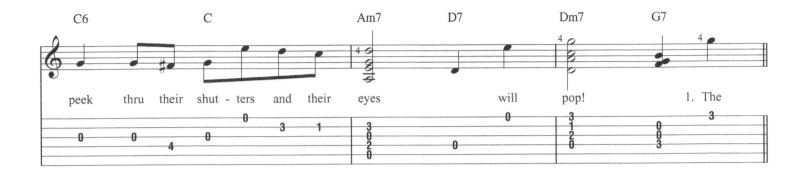

peek thru their shut - ters and their eyes will pop! 1. The

Bridge

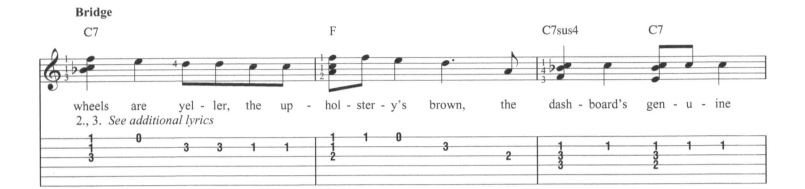

wheels are yel - ler, the up - hol - ster - y's brown, the dash - board's gen - u - ine
2., 3. *See additional lyrics*

leath - er, with Is - in - glass cur - tains y' can roll right down, in

Verse

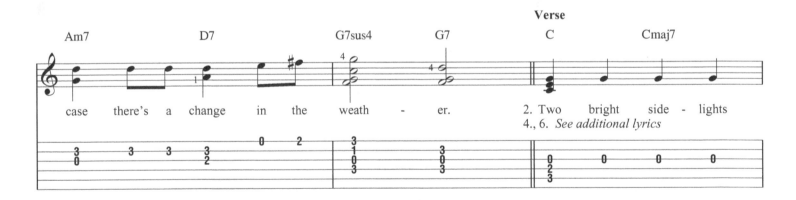

case there's a change in the weath - er. 2. Two bright side - lights
4., 6. *See additional lyrics*

wink - in' and blink - in', ain't no fin - er rig, I'm a think - in'.

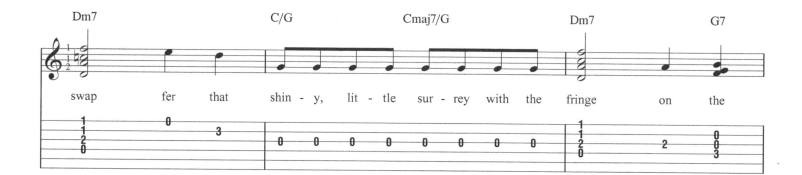

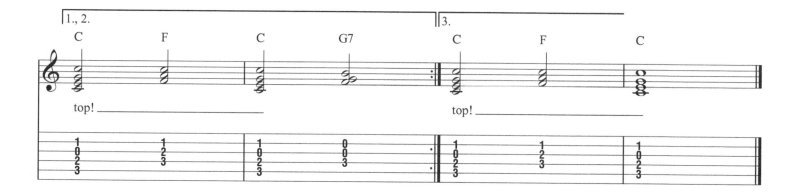

Additional Lyrics

3. All the world'll fly in a flurry when I take you out in the surrey,
When I take you out in the surrey with the fringe on top!
When we hit that road, hell fer leather, cats and dogs'll dance in the heather,
Birds and frogs'll sing all together and the toads will hop!

Bridge 2 The winds will whistle as we rattle along, the cows'll moo in the clover,
The river will ripple out a whispered song, and whisper it over and over.

4. Don't you wisht y'd go on forever? Don't you wisht y'd go on forever?
Don't you wisht y'd go on forever and ud never stop
In that shiny, little surrey with the fringe on the top!

5. I can see the stars gettin' blurry when we drive back home in the surrey,
Drivin' slowly home in the surrey with the fringe on top!
I can feel the day gettin' older, feel a sleepy head on my shoulder,
Noddin', droopin' close to my shoulder till it falls kerplop!

Bridge 3 The sun is swimmin' on the rim of the hill, the moon is takin' a header,
And jist as I'm thinkin' all the earth is still, a lark'll wake up in the medder.

6. Hush, you bird, my baby's a sleepin'! Maybe got a dream worth a keepin'.
Whoa! You team, and jist keep a creepin' at a slow clip clop.
Don't you hurry with the surrey with the fringe on the top!

Waltz for Debby

Lyric by Gene Lees
Music by Bill Evans

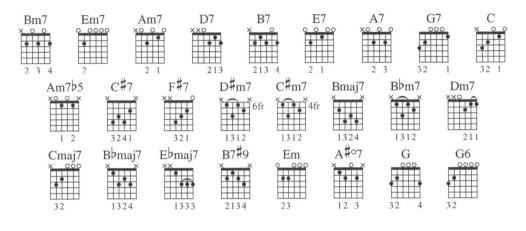

Strum Pattern: 7
Pick Pattern: 7

Verse
Slow, in 1

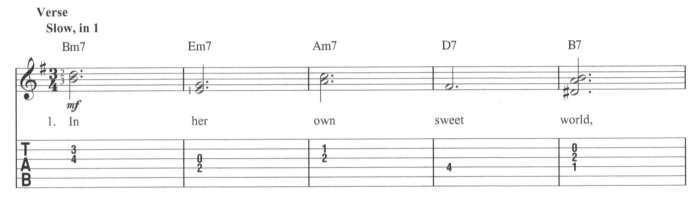

1. In her own sweet world,

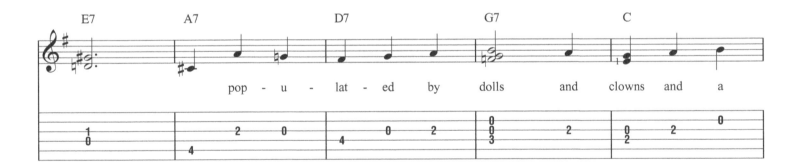

pop - u - lat - ed by dolls and clowns and a

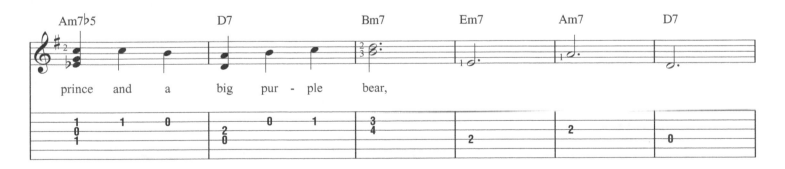

prince and a big pur - ple bear,

Sweet Georgia Brown

Words and Music by Ben Bernie, Maceo Pinkard and Kenneth Casey

Strum Pattern: 5
Pick Pattern: 5

Verse

2. It's been said she knocks 'em dead ___ when she lands in town. ___
4. All those tips the por - ter slips ___ to Sweet Geor - gia Brown, ___

___ Since she came, why it's a shame ___ how she cools 'em down. ___
___ they buy clothes at fash - ion shows ___ with one dol - lar down. ___

___ Fel - lers ___ she can't get ___ are fel - lers ___
___ Oh boy, ___ tip your hats; ___ oh joy, ___

she ain't met. ___ Geor - gia claimed ___ her, Geor - gia named ___ her
she's the "cat's." ___ Who's that, mis - ter? 'Tain't her sis - ter,

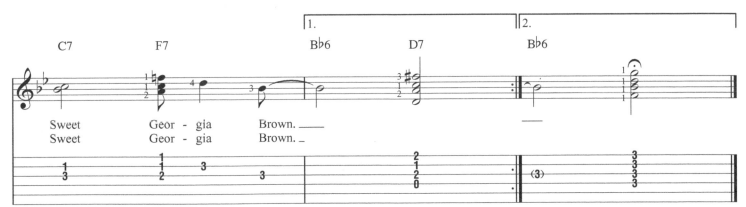

Sweet Geor - gia Brown. ___
Sweet Geor - gia Brown. ___

Taking a Chance on Love

Words by John La Touche and Ted Fetter
Music by Vernon Duke

Strum Pattern: 5
Pick Pattern: 1

Verse lyrics:
1. Here I go a-gain, ___ I hear those trum-pets blow a-gain, ___
3., 5. *See additional lyrics*

all a - glow a - gain, ___ tak - ing a chance on love.

Here I slide a - gain, ___ a - bout to take that ride a - gain, ___

star - ry - eyed a - gain, ___ tak - ing a chance on love. 1. I

Bridge

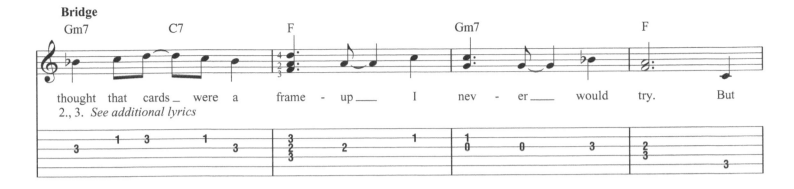

thought that cards _ were a frame - up ___ I nev - er ___ would try. But

2., 3. *See additional lyrics*

now I'm tak - ing the game up ___ and the ace of hearts is high.

Verse

2. Things are mend - ing now, _ I see a rain - bow blend - ing now, _

4., 6. *See additional lyrics*

we'll have our hap - py end - ing now, _ tak - ing a chance on love. love.

Additional Lyrics

3. Here I come again,
   I'm gonna make things hum again,
   Acting dumb again,
   Taking a chance on love.
   Here I stand again,
   About to beat the band again,
   Feeling grand again,
   Taking a chance on love.

Bridge 2 I never dreamed in my slumbers,
   And bets were taboo.
   But now I'm playing at the numbers
   On a little dream for two.

4. Wading in again,
   I'm leading with my chin again,
   I'm startin' out to win again,
   Taking a chance on love.

5. Here I slip again,
   About to take that trip again,
   Got my grip again,
   Taking a chance on love.
   Now I prove again
   That I can make life move again,
   In the groove again,
   Taking a chance on love.

Bridge 3 I walk around with a horseshoe,
   In clover I lie.
   And Brother Rabbit, of course you
   Better kiss your foot goodbye.

6. On the ball again,
   I'm ridin' for a fall again,
   I'm gonna give my all again,
   Taking a chance on love.

Tea for Two

from NO, NO, NANETTE

Words by Irving Caesar
Music by Vincent Youmans

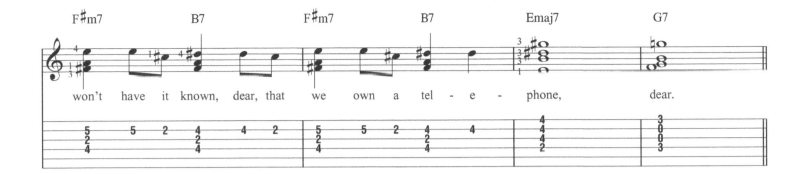

won't have it known, dear, that we own a tel - e - phone, dear.

Verse

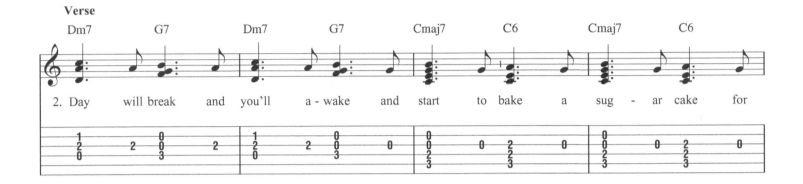

2. Day will break and you'll a - wake and start to bake a sug - ar cake for

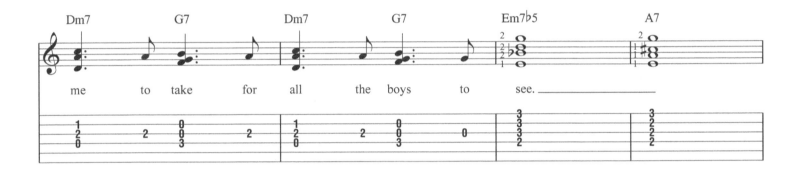

me to take for all the boys to see. _____

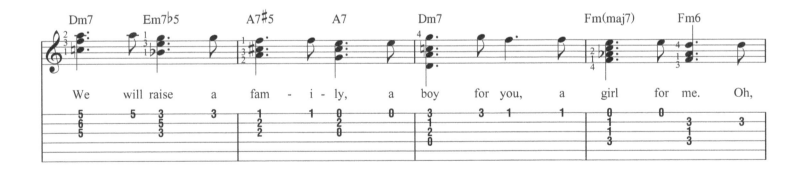

We will raise a fam - i - ly, a boy for you, a girl for me. Oh,

can't you see how hap - py we would be? _____

That's All

Words and Music by Bob Haymes and Alan E. Brandt

told you they would give you the world for a toy. All I

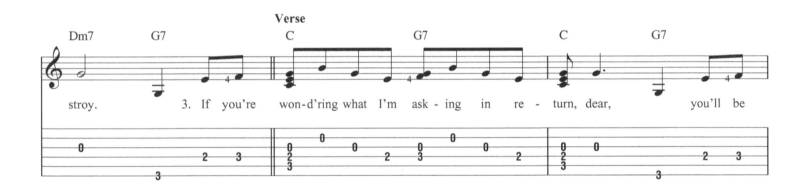

have are these arms to en - fold you and a love time can nev - er de -

Verse

stroy. 3. If you're won-d'ring what I'm ask - ing in re - turn, dear, you'll be

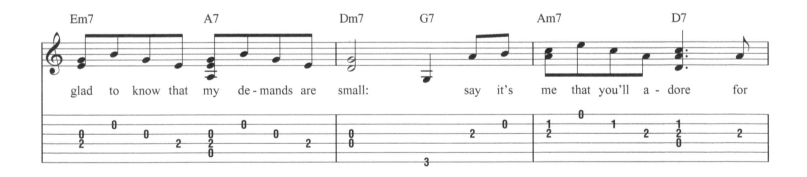

glad to know that my de - mands are small: say it's me that you'll a - dore for

now and ev - er - more. That's all, that's all.

What Is This Thing Called Love?

from WAKE UP AND DREAM
Words and Music by Cole Porter

Strum Pattern: 5
Pick Pattern: 1

Verse
Moderately fast

1. What is this thing called love?

This fun - ny thing called

love? Just who can solve

its mys - ter - y? Why

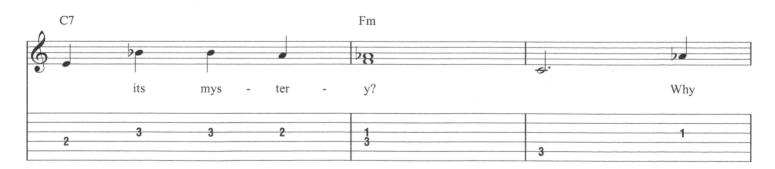

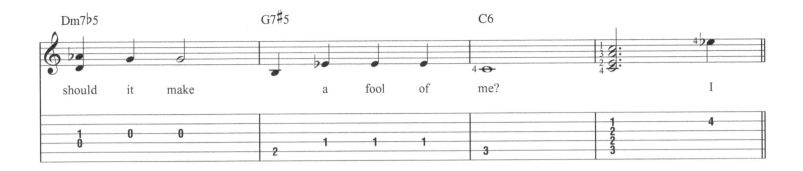

Bridge

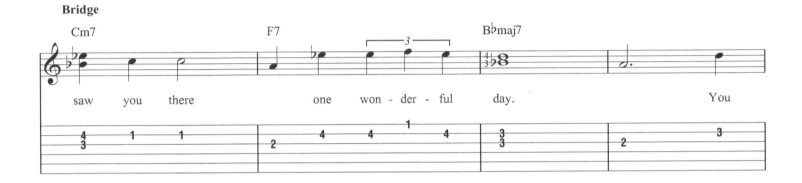

Verse

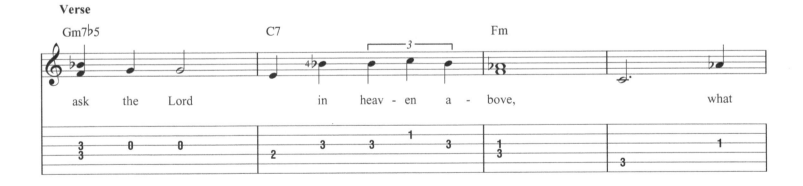

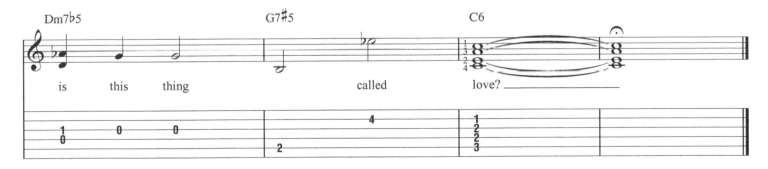

121

When I Fall in Love

from ONE MINUTE TO ZERO

Words by Edward Heyman
Music by Victor Young

Strum Pattern: 3
Pick Pattern: 1

Verse
Moderately slow

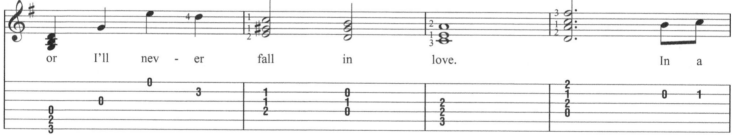

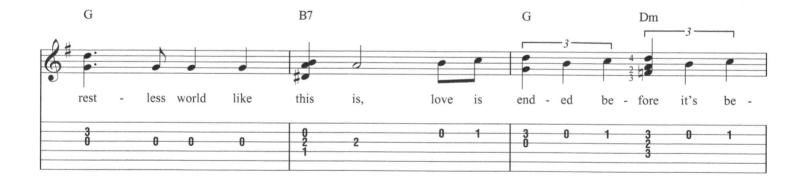

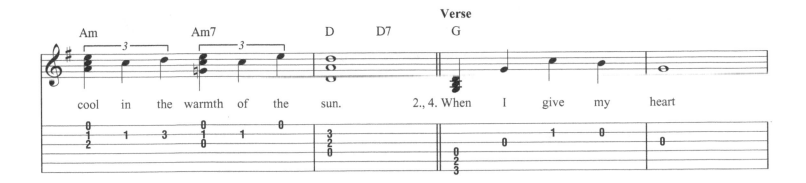

cool   in   the   warmth   of   the   sun.   2., 4. When   I   give   my   heart

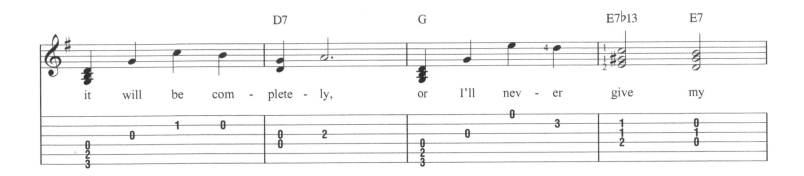

it   will   be   com - plete - ly,   or   I'll   nev - er   give   my

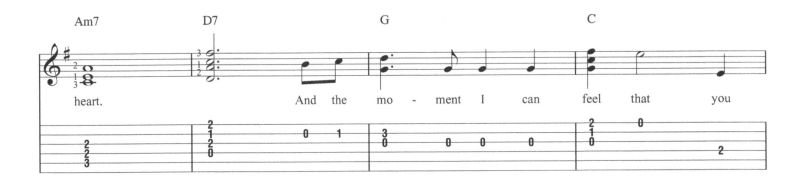

heart.   And   the   mo - ment   I   can   feel   that   you

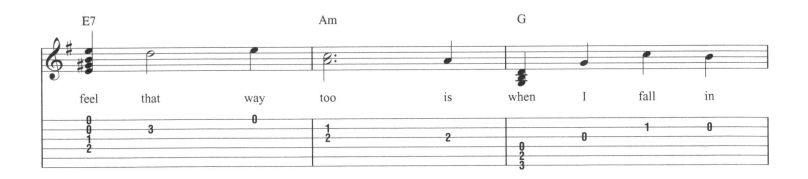

feel   that   way   too   is   when   I   fall   in

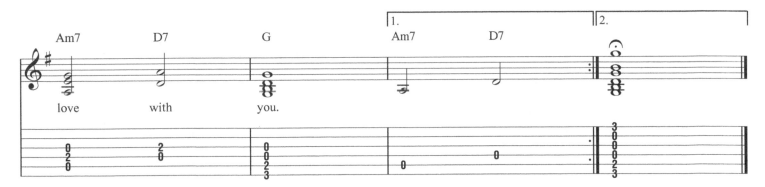

love   with   you.

You and the Night and the Music

from REVENGE WITH MUSIC

Words by Howard Dietz
Music by Arthur Schwartz

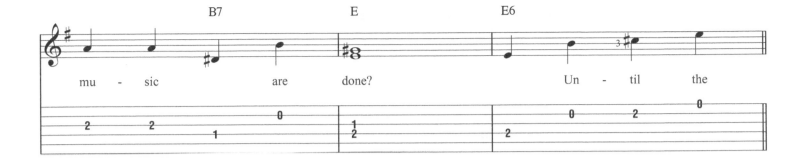

mu - sic are done? Un - til the

Bridge

pale light of dawn - ing and day - light, our hearts will be throb - bing gui - tars.

Morn - ing may come with - out warn - ing, and take a - way the stars.

Verse

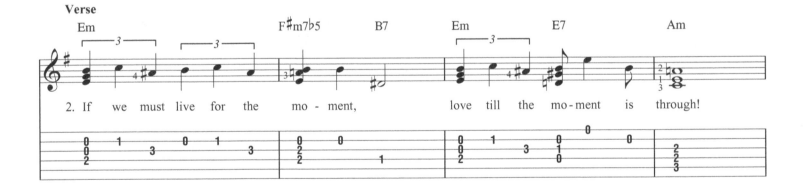

2. If we must live for the mo - ment, love till the mo - ment is through!

Af - ter the night and the mu - sic die, will I have you?

You Stepped Out of a Dream

from the M-G-M Picture ZIEGFELD GIRL

Words by Gus Kahn
Music by Nacio Herb Brown

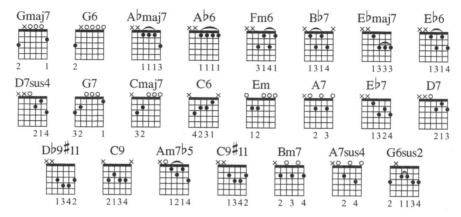

Strum Pattern: 3
Pick Pattern: 3

Verse
Moderately slow, in 2

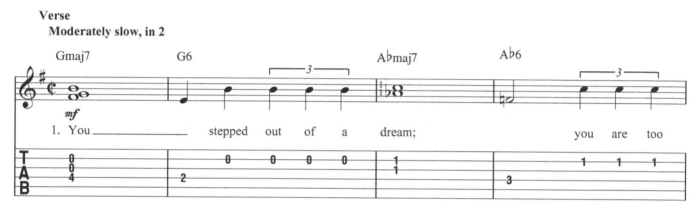

1. You _____ stepped out of a dream; you are too

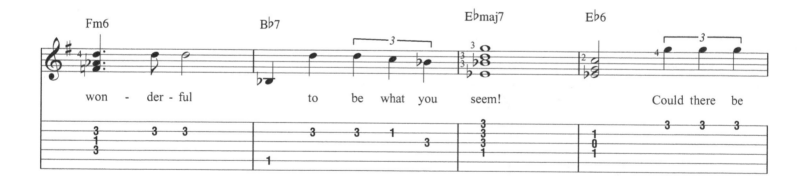

won - der - ful to be what you seem! Could there be

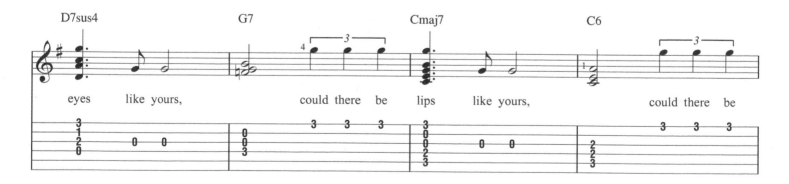

eyes like yours, could there be lips like yours, could there be

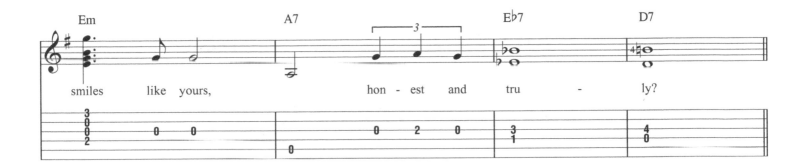

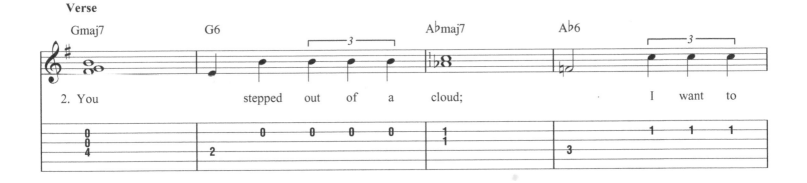

Verse

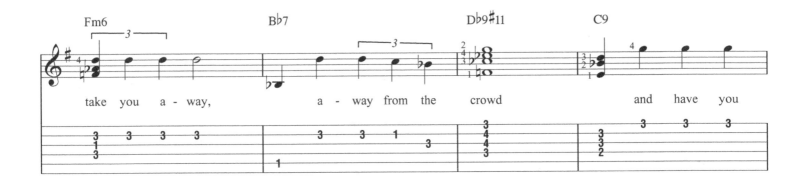

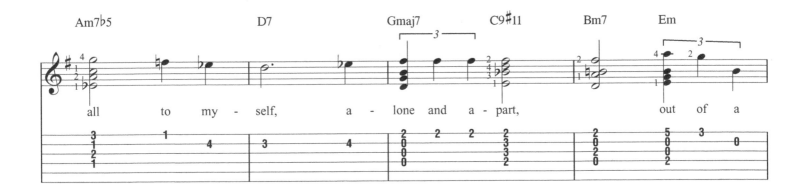

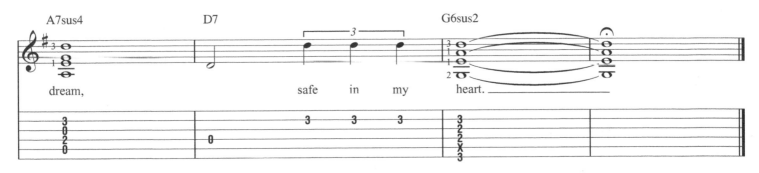

STRUM AND PICK PATTERNS

This chart contains the suggested strum and pick patterns that are referred to by number at the beginning
of each song in this book. The symbols ⊓ and ∨ in the strum patterns refer to down and up strokes, respectively.
The letters in the pick patterns indicate which right-hand fingers play which strings.

p = thumb
i = index finger
m = middle finger
a = ring finger

For example; Pick Pattern 2
is played: thumb - index - middle - ring

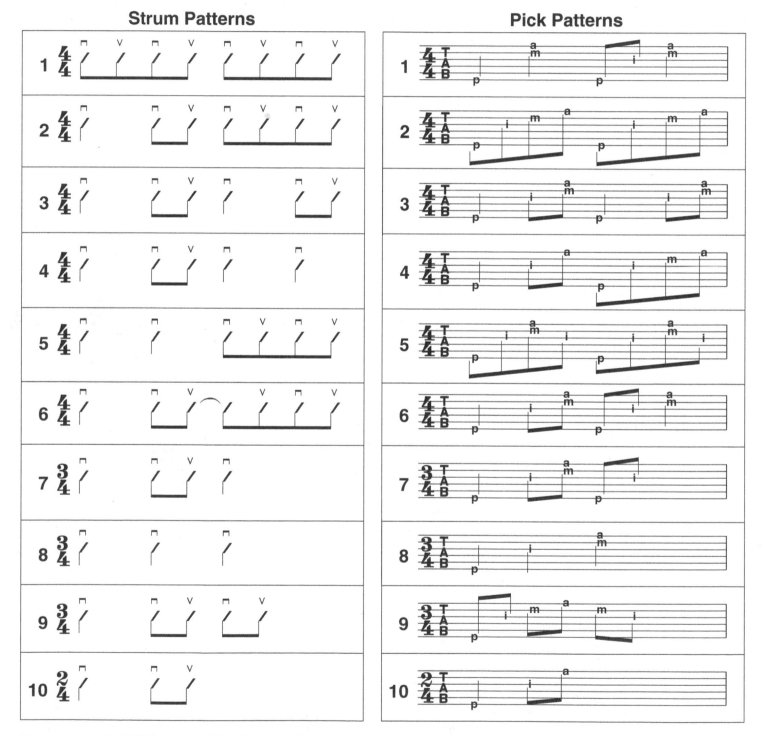

You can use the 3/4 Strum and Pick Patterns in songs written in compound meter (6/8, 9/8, 12/8, etc.).
For example, you can accompany a song in 6/8 by playing the 3/4 pattern twice in each measure.
The 4/4 Strum and Pick Patterns can be used for songs written in cut time (¢) by doubling the note
time values in the patterns. Each pattern would therefore last two measures in cut time.